THERE ARE NO ACCIDENTS
IN LOVE AND RELATIONSHIPS

Meaningful Coincidences and
the Stories of Our Families

by

Robert H. Hopcke

CHIRON PUBLICATIONS • ASHEVILLE, NORTH CAROLINA

www.ChironPublications.com

Interior and cover design by Danijela Mijailović
Printed primarily in the United States of America.

ISBN 978-1-63051-488-4 paperback
ISBN 978-1-63051-489-1 hardcover
ISBN 978-1-63051-490-7 electronic
ISBN 978-1-63051-491-4 limited edition paperback

Library of Congress Cataloging-in-Publication Data

Names: Hopcke, Robert H., 1958- author.
Title: There are no accidents in love and relationships : meaningful
   coincidences and the stories of our families / by Robert H. Hopcke.
Description: Asheville : Chiron Publications, [2018] | Includes
   bibliographical references and index.
Identifiers: LCCN 2018000784| ISBN 9781630514884 (pbk. : alk. paper) |
   ISBN 9781630514891 (hardcover : alk. paper)
Subjects: LCSH: Coincidence. | Friendship. | Families--Psychological
   aspects. Jungian psychology.
Classification: LCC BF1175 .H67 2018 | DDC 155.2--dc23
LC record available at https://lccn.loc.gov/2018000784

"Sometimes the best families are the ones God builds using unexpected pieces of our hearts." Melanie Shankle, *Sparkly Green Earrings: Catching the Light at Every Turn*

Table of Contents

Preface

When my first book on synchronicity *There Are No Accidents: Synchronicity and the Stories of Our Lives* appeared now almost 20 years ago, in 1997, I would not have said that this concept of meaningful coincidences was entirely unknown to the general public. In the course of the interviews and research I did back then, it was pretty clear that this idea of C. G. Jung's, first coined in the 1950s, had made its way into the consciousness and vocabulary of mostly everyone I had spoken to, so that when I solicited stories from people about the synchronistic events that had changed their lives, I really didn't have to explain what the book was going to be about (though, somewhat humorously, I did often have to explain that Sting and the Police did not coin the term with their album *Synchronicity* but he had, for all its creativity, originally gotten the word from Jung.)

The truth is, however, that the general notion of meaningful chance goes by a number of different names. Serendipity is most frequently the synonym that comes to people's mind, a term with an even more venerable history than Jung's, dating back to a Horace Walpole story published first in 1754 which itself was based on an even older Persian folktale, *The Princes of Serendip*. But in the ensuing years of my lecturing about synchronicity as Jung intended the concept, it came to my attention that many of the ways people thought, spoke about or used the concept they were ostensibly calling "synchronicity" differed sometimes a little, and sometimes a lot, from what Jung himself meant. I would often hear people equating synchronicity with ideas of "fate" or "destiny" or "cosmic connection"—all perfectly understandable ways of trying to make sense of often quite dramatic, wholly unexpected and indeed frequently unintended and even unwelcome coincidences—but none of these are, in fact, "synchronicity." Other people, of a more rationalistic or scientific bent, would find themselves looking toward elements, properties or characteristics of the physical world being discovered through subatomic research or innovations in post-Newtonian physics, so as to explain such seemingly random coincidences lived out on the macro level of our experience, but the so-called "unified field" or "the uncertainty principle" are not really "synchronicity" in its original sense either.

As I said, both directions of these sorts of thoughts have merit in their own right, but Jung's own idea of synchronicity is fundamentally quite different. Being first and foremost a practicing, clinical psychiatrist, C. G. Jung published *Synchronicity: An Acausal Connecting Principle* in 1950 in order to advance the term he coined for it as a *psychological* principle. He was interested throughout his career, and in particular, with how people made meaning in their lives, from the inside out, so to speak, describing our interior experience not narrowly as just "mind" but instead adopting the much more comprehensive and resonant Greek word, "psyche," which he then used interchangeably throughout his writings with the vernacular word, "soul." Therefore, I've often said in my talks and classes on synchronicity that just about everything you need to know about Jung's concept is actually right there in the title of his book. He coined the concept of synchronicity because he was driven throughout his life to understand how we human beings make *connections*—how our unconscious life is connected to our conscious life (or not, in the case of psychological illness); how our past—personal and collective—is connected to the present moment of consciousness in service of a movement forward into a future of greater integration (or, again, not, for those suffering from emotional difficulties or trauma); and finally, how our inward lives—perhaps the most intimate and ultimately un-shareable level of experience, our subjectivity— nevertheless reaches up and out to meet and bond with the lives of others around us, first our parents, then our families, and then our ever expanding circles of friends, acquaintances and even society at large. Synchronicity isn't outside us in a supernatural fate or in the physical world of subatomic fields: it is within us. In Jung's thought, synchronicity is a principle of *psychological connection*.

Both the metaphysical and the scientific views in fact seek to explain the power of the events on the basis of their causes. If an apparent coincidence is "fate," then an objective realm of spirit lies behind the predetermined path being disclosed to us in the events that happen, over which, arguably, as fate, we have no say or influence. Likewise, if strange and uncanny coincidences occur to us on the larger level of our lives, the idea that this is in the end because all matter is somehow essentially "unified," or that on some level of physical existence separation is merely "apparent," is to posit a causal explanation for the event. Neither form of explanation, however, even if true, was Jung's focus or intention. And indeed, as I think I've made clear, the wise old man of Bollingen was perfectly content to call the coincidences *a-causal*, that is to say, instances of random chance, and devote his attention instead to the connection between inward state and outward circumstance that these unique, sometimes delightful, sometimes upsetting, coincidences bring forward within us.

Having made a bit of career so far in my writing on synchronicity to make clear the authentic character of Jung's idea of synchronicity as a psychological principle, my intention is to continue to do so here with my second book, which examines synchronicity in the context of the story of our families. In *There Are No Accidents*, I took a broader view of the topic and looked at all the various areas of our lives in which synchronistic events are prone to occur: our love lives—how people met their life partners, how relationships changed or even ended; our work life—how those I interviewed found a job or ended up in their career, by way of unintended but meaningful chance events; our inner lives, as evidenced by synchronistic dreams and spiritual or religious occurrences, such as meeting one's spiritual teacher or those sponta-neous events of healing or transformation we generally call "miracles;" and then finally stories of synchronicity occurring around the two transitions every human being makes—our birth and our death.

In doing the research for *There Are No Accidents*, I had the distinct delight to speak with probably close to 100 or so people about how synchronistic events had led them to their spouse or ended an unfulfilling job in order to make way for a new and more satisfying career or had, by complete chance, wrought an interior spiritual transformation. However, there was an entire class of story that at the time of my writing I hadn't anticipated and didn't neatly fit into the outline of the book I had planned. And yet, by the end of my interviews for the first book, I found myself with an abundant and quite a wonderful collection of intriguing and thought-provoking stories that I felt quite frankly deserved a book of their own: family stories. Now, of course, these experiences of connections between family members makes sense after all, since each of our families is in a way a universe unto itself and certainly for every one of us an inexhaustible fund of meaning and insight, the foundation of our being.

But, even after 35 years of practice as a marriage and family therapist, I have to confess that as I finally prepared to take on this long-planned book concerning synchronicity and the stories of our families, I felt quite daunted by how even to begin. What does "family" even mean? Do I address the biological aspect of what a family is, the raw, basic physico-genetic basis of our familial connections? I could, but, as we all know, particularly in the modern era with all our previous notions about "family" in full-fledged transformation, it is no longer valid to define "family" in such a reductive fashion alone (if it ever was). As any of us can attest, I daresay, "blood" relatives with every biological connection possible, right on down to identical twinship, might have nothing to do with one another, whereas people with precisely no biological connection to one another might well be or become the closest of "family." In fact, when you think about it, any couple at all that comes to together are indeed—in fact, socially and even legally, have to be—biological strangers to one another before uniting lovingly and physically to create a relationship and subsequently a family of their own.

For this reason, I think it is important to start a book of synchronistic stories concerning family relationships with the frank acknowledgement that here I will definitely *not* be emphasizing the sheer biological nature of family. Now, given the nature of discourse concerning what the family is or should be in certain quarters of our society these days, I am aware that to consider the family beyond the mechanics of genetic transmission is, for some people, a radical transgression, religious anathema, and often a profound, even cosmological, threat. To which I say: so be it, or, as the young people put it these days, "Whatever. Good luck with that!"

So, beyond this narrow biological discourse, though, I feel confident stating that the great majority of us know full well that what constitutes a "family." Those whom we consider part of our own "family" may have a biological relationship to us of some sort, but they occupy that space in our lives and our hearts we call our family because of a wealth of other reasons. And it is this fuller concept of family that, as a psychotherapist and a Jungian, I actually found the far more interesting aspect of the stories I heard. The synchronistic events people told me about which are the origin of this book—random chance but profoundly meaningful connections between loved ones—made clear that the family is, above all, a psychological experience.

To call the family a psychological experience is to cover a *lot* of ground using a single word, for our psyche is, arguably, its own world, which means that our psychological experience of family is a bit like a kaleidoscope with myriad parts of ourselves and our relationships, changing, coming and going. The family is in this way an *emotional reality*, constituted by how we feel and who we feel close to and bonded with according to our basic capacity for and styles of attachment. Born out of such attachments, starting with our primary caregiver—mother most frequently, father likewise as important in a different way—and then their relatives and our siblings, the emotional nature at the heart of our family experience becomes elaborated into a *social reality*, arguably the basic unit of society itself. And therefore, going further still, tilting the kaleidoscope of our view on the family to reveal yet another aspect, as a social unit, the family becomes, of course, a *historical reality*. We each know this ourselves personally, since all of us are the latest in a long series of ancestors, and with the advent of the Internet as well as advances in genetic testing, DNA analysis and the like, this peculiarly historical dimension of our families has given rise to a genuine surge of interest in genealogy. In seeking an answer to the perennial psychological question, "Who am I?" many of us have picked up this historical aspect of what a family is to find out where and who we came from, what branch, twig, and leaf of the family tree do we represent.

And yet, perhaps at the risk of contradicting myself, I believe in using the psychological lens here to look at what the family does include—indeed, maybe even *must* take into account—the biological aspects of our family connection. However, even these physical, genetic connections, I would argue, aren't simply factual data. When I say, "I have my mother's eyes," or "all us Smiths are short in stature" or "my brothers and I all are gifted in sports," we are noting the physical connections because of what these resemblances *mean* to us. Even what we share biologically becomes part of a psychological narrative that we then construct about who we are in the world. Ironically perhaps, it is then the biological aspect of family which brings us back to the notion of synchronicity as meaningful chance. After all, is there anything more random, more open to chance, less causal and determined than the sheer genetic combinations that come together to bring us literally into existence? I think not. Every conception, every birth, every single one of us is, so to speak, a unique and unrepeatable synchronicity—the manifestation in our person of an acausal connection, in this case of ineffable, spiral strands of DNA, of chromosomes coming together by chance.

The kaleidoscopic nature of family is slowly what became clear for me, piece by piece, as I heard stories of ways in which synchronicity was experienced specifically within the ambit of people's families. So, the stories I was privileged to hear ended up serving as excellent illustrations of the essentially psychological aspect of synchronicity. They, in turn, threw a light on the fundamentally psychological quality of what constitutes a "family," the meaning of which I felt very strongly was an eminently healthy thing to explore fully and to assert forthrightly in the face of many reductive definitions of family afoot in the world today.

The stories I heard about the way synchronistic events shaped people's families and their experience of belonging in the world fall into three broad categories: past, present, and future. Likewise, I have let these categories shape this book.

Our family constitutes our past, the ground of our being, our origins. Synchronistic events often bring our conscious attention to aspects of this source of our being and grounding in the world about which we are unconscious, and many emphasize the complex nature of relationship as something that is often discovered or found, rather than intentionally created or sought. Thus, the family represents in a way our historical self, and the stories that follow show how chance events can disclose features of that history in ways that enlarge and even complete our sense of self. How I met my spouse, startling coincidences that bring forth commonalities with ancestors or historical events, ways in which we ourselves recover parts of our own childhood through a synchronistic occurrence, dream or vision—all these connect us to our family's place in the sweep of time.

Our families are our present: through meaningful coincidences, we are often woken up to the strength or character of the deep bond we have with our parents, siblings and relatives through symbolic connections and uncanny, shared experiences that go beyond rational explanation or conscious intention. Such events strengthen our sense of belonging or show us how our family isn't just a place of origin but an aspect of who we are.

And, of course, in the end, our families also represent our future—the part of us that, because of its collective and archetypal nature, transcends death and time, that which brought us into being and that which continues about us even past our passing out of this life. Synchronistic events, as I will be discussing here, most often pop up at times of transitions in our lives, and there are no two more important transitions for us human beings than the transition into and out of this life. The circumstances of our own birth and the birth of those we love, I found, were occasions of richly meaningful synchronicities, and, naturally, the transition out of this life, particularly our experience of the death of a loved one, likewise were full of coincidence and emotion.

In the original book I wrote, my focus was to bring forward the depth and complexity of Jung's concept of synchronicity and to make clear what his original intention for this notion was (or was not). The stories in that book, therefore, covered a wide variety of synchronistic events, both in character, type and significance, and all were intended to illustrate the scope of Jung's concept for the reader. In this book, however, I found myself in a way naturally inverting the emphasis between story and concept, and, because it is the second book on this topic I'm writing—one that centers really upon a very specific type of synchronistic event—I felt drawn to let people's stories occupy more of the focus themselves. I wanted to let these family tales have the fuller and deeper space they required and to use Jung's concept of syn-chronicity to punctuate what made these meaningful coincidences in people's lives so significant to them. For those interested in a bit more of a psychological exposition of the concept itself, *There Are No Accidents* stands to provide the more complete presentation of this original idea, whereas in this present book, family stories take center stage. I think in some ways my choice to go into more depth about the larger context in which a family synchronicity occurred is more suited to the topic of synchronicity itself. Because what is meaningful to you or me is an intensely subjective, inward, almost indescribable experience at times, it often happens that a quick and cursory telling of a synchronistic event leaves one wondering why such a coincidence had the impact it did. So, in this book, I decided to let the story itself make the point about its significance, to illustrate the synchronicity in a way that brought forward, to the best of my ability as a writer and psychologist, the inward experience of how and why a chance event ended up changing our sense of family and thus, also, our own sense of self.

CHAPTER ONE

Enlightened by Chance-A Brief Introduction to Jung's Notion of Synchronicity

I was adopted at birth, and I suppose like all families, my adoptive parents—whom I simply call my parents—repeatedly told a bit of story about their bringing me home from the hospital in Jersey City when I was three days old. They had waited some time for the adoption to be arranged through Lutheran Social Services and on the day in mid-March when I was to come home, there was a tremendous blizzard, making the roads dangerous, if not impassable, and thus putting the whole event in jeopardy. There were, of course, quite a few old-timey Polaroids of that day that I grew up seeing as accompaniment to this bit of family lore about the blizzard, handed around and posing with my grandparents and my dad in front of the picture window in our living room, beyond which you could see the waist-high drifts of snow. But home I came, nevertheless, to the Hopckes as a Hopcke, and the circumstances as narrated by my parents had a little bit of the "neither rain nor sleet nor hail nor snow nor dead of night...." quality to it, with the implication that it was as if I had been snatched up and rescued from elements on a doorstep, though the adoption was very by the book and, in fact, pretty uneventful.

I grew up knowing I was adopted; indeed, I was reading by age three and one of the first books I had was entitled "The Chosen Baby" (it may well still be in a box somewhere at my sister's house) and was written to explain adoption to adopted children. Occasionally childhood friends of mine would inquire as to what I knew about my "other parents." I do remember my friend Stephanie spinning out a rather tragically dramatic tale about how they might have died in a fire, my father attempting to save my mother by climbing through a second-story window and yet failing and perishing himself. All fanciful, of course, but in reality, despite the normal conflicts that occur in any family and particular differences in personality and temperament, my upbringing was altogether stable and suburban, and my relationship with my parents quite close and good. So, for most of my life, I really had no curiosity about my birth parents, not as a child, nor as an adolescent, nor even during college.

In eighth grade, I took French and got myself a pen pal of the same age who lived outside of Paris with whom I corresponded faithfully and frequently, and at the end of the year, his family invited me to come stay with them, which I did at age 14. One soaks up a foreign language like a sponge at that age anyway. Plus, his family spoke no English—an experience of pure linguistic immersion—not to mention, I seemed right from an early age to have a special aptitude for language, reading early, already writing short stories and poetry in third grade. So, I returned from my time in France fluent at age 14, and decided that, sure, I could sail through another four years of high school French, or I could challenge myself, which was why I decided to take Italian, as well.

If you had asked me, I wouldn't have been able to say why Italian and not Spanish. Spanish would have made as much sense, as a cognate Romance language, and surely would have been more useful given the demographics of the United States. But there was something about Italian, and Italians, for which I had always felt a particular affinity. Unusually for a public high school, our Italian teacher was herself a native Italian, and anywhere from half to three-quarters of students who took Italian in our high school were themselves either immigrants or the children of immigrants. After my summer in France, I enjoyed the French language and culture, but I *loved* Italian--the music of the language, the emotional resonance, the extraversion of the cultural style. So, from then on, I was like the boy in the film *Breaking Away*, a kid with a German last name who looked, acted, and now even spoke and sung Italian, such that for the many close friends I made with the other Italian kids in my class and their families, I was soon, inevitably, rechristened "Roberto."

Speaking French and Italian fluently by the time I went to college, therefore, I attended Georgetown where those two languages became my double major, and in my junior year abroad, I spent the year enrolled as an Italian student in the Facoltà di Filosofie e Lettere at the University of Florence. There was a bit of the academic-linguistic boot camp experience about that year, since there we all were, American students dropped in from a different country and a wholly different educational system, side by side with Italian university students in courses on art history, Italian literature and European history, at a level that would have been more or less equivalent scholastically to the first or second year of American graduate studies, with of course, all the lectures, all the discussions, all the tutoring and all the readings completely in Italian. Deep immersion: sink or swim.

But in Italy, I soon found, I didn't just swim. I thrived. As with high school, there was something about being in Italy that simply "fit" me, and in fact, once I had traded my American clothes for then contemporary Italian/European styles, by the end of that year, especially when traveling around the south of Italy, I was often mistaken for Italian. They could hear a slight accent or intonation when I opened my mouth, but with my thick dark curly hair, my acquired Italian body language (hand gestures and various faces are indispensable parts of any conversation—some stereotypes are based on the truth), and my educated fluency in speaking and thorough familiarity with the culture after over a year living there, most southern Italians would often just assume I was a *paesano* of the north.

A watershed year it was for me, life-changing, and though I didn't pursue an academic career in French or Italian, I ended up tutoring

Italian and doing private translation work as a way to earn money during my grad school years in California. My partner and eventual husband Paul had lived in Montreal, spoke French fluently himself, and had a grand appreciation for Europe and Italy, so that during the course of our relationship, pretty much every other year, we would visit either France or Italy or both, often staying with my friends in Rome that I maintained my relationships with since the time I had lived in Florence. Thus, Italy was a part of who I was.

The reader might well be thinking at this point—as I am myself, as I look back on this story—"why did he not simply consider the obvious?" Adopted child, clear affinities, actual physical characteristics, speaks Italian fluently and easily, various seemingly random choices and experiences consistently reinforcing a relationship to Italy and to Italian culture that grew more multi-layered and richer every year. What was going on with me looks pretty clear, in retrospect. But in large part out of unconscious solicitude for my parents' feelings, it really wasn't until a long and persistent series of dreams about my birth parents occurred during Jungian analysis in my mid-20s—birth parents who were always and without exception Italian or Italian American in these dreams—that my analyst gently but repeatedly raised the issue. "I think your unconscious is telling you it is time to find out about your birth parents." And after some resistance to the idea, I finally came to agree that he was right.

When I hear about the difficulties confronted by other adoptees in finding their birth parents, I am a little stunned that for me it was so easy. In the first place, the social worker at Lutheran Social Services who had handled my adoption 27 years previously was still working at LSS when I contacted them, and she remembered both my adoption as well as my parents quite vividly. (Thirty-five years into my own career as a psychotherapist, I now completely understand how this could be the case, for I would have absolutely no problem remembering a client I had seen during my internship 30 years ago.) She suggested I start by reviewing the non-identifying information that was available to me without the necessity of any sort of consent on anyone's part, and so, not surprisingly, when that information arrived, I received confirmation of what I had on some level come to know about myself: my birth mother was Italian-American. There was very little information about my birth father which, she explained, was because the records showed he had not been involved in the process of my adoption.

However, because I spoke Italian, lived and studied in Italy, and constantly traveled to Italy, I realized almost immediately that, far from closing the issue, I suddenly felt a rather powerful need to know where my family was specifically from. In part, this was due to the particular nature of Italy itself, which as an integrated nation, is of relatively recent historical vintage. Italians do indeed see themselves as Italian in nationality, but the long regional histories of the various provinces as independent nations, duchies, and kingdoms in their own right means that every Italian carries around a very strong regional identity as well. So, too, for me, it wasn't enough to know that I was Italian in some general way; I also needed to know where I was from, where my people were from, where my ancestral history was specifically and particularly located.

Unfortunately, when I finally got around to recontacting the agency about that even more fine detail about my background, the social worker I had been dealing with had retired and had been replaced with a gentleman whose clinical manner was bureaucratic, cold and pretty unresponsive. "No, there's no information on that. No, I don't know where or how you could get it. I could look further, but I have your file here and there's nothing in it." At this point, I was already a licensed marriage and family therapist here in California, running my own practice as well as an AIDS prevention program in San Francisco, supervising interns, with two published books. So, the immovable bureaucratic object of his indifference was about to meet the unstoppable force of my determination to get my own history and to be treated with the kind of clinical respect and responsiveness to which I felt entitled. I pushed, and eventually he said that the only way to get the particular information about my Italian background I was seeking would be to institute a search for my birth mother with a view toward direct contact, which would cost $300 and which the agency would pursue on my behalf.

At the time, I was somewhat incensed to discover that a full-fledged professional adult had to jump through so many hoops simply to obtain his own history. I'm happy to say that attitudes have evolved so that, now, the rights and entitlements of adopted children to that history have increased in importance with respect to the rights and entitlements of the adopted and birth parents. Having to pay an agency $300 to get something to which I felt morally and emotionally entitled—my own ancestral history—didn't sit well with me. But there we were, so pay I did.

So far, I think it's already synchronistic enough of a story that I, with absolutely no knowledge of my Italian heritage nor even any real curiosity throughout my life about whatever heritage I might have by birth, would emerge into adulthood so thoroughly identified with Italian culture, speaking the language, living in the country, only to find out that—yes, indeed!—I am actually of Italian descent and didn't know it. But the story does get better, and were it not for an even more dramatic synchronistic event in the form of a dream, there might not have been any conclusion to my quest for full knowledge about where my family came from.

Months went by and I heard nothing from the agency, until the issue began to heat up a bit for me. Paul and I had planned to spend the month of August in Italy that year. So, I wanted to know by then where my family was from, because I would surely want to visit the town or towns while we were there. It was about a month before we were due to leave, and one night, preoccupied as I was with the issue, I had a very simple dream: a female voice said to me, the way an angel might, "Your mother's name is Gloria." I woke up, struck by the power of the dream's stark simplicity, and thought, well, sure. Because in fact my mother's name was Gloria, Gloria Hopcke. I remembered discussing it in analysis, but because my mother's name was Gloria, all we really made of it was to see it as confirmatory dream, one which reinforced the emotional rightness of what I was doing by pushing to get the information about my family background that I was seeking.

As time was growing short before we were to leave for Italy, I made quite a few phone calls to the agency. In reply, the social worker left only a vague message that they were looking into the matter but hadn't found anything. But then, the week before we were due to take off, I had finally reached the end of my patience. I called the agency, quite angry, insisted on waiting on hold until the social worker was available to talk to me, and when he got on the phone, I frankly grilled him as to what they had done for the $300 to actually locate my birth mother. He hemmed and hawed, really couldn't give many specifics, until finally I said, "Look it, I know you have the identifying information sitting right there in the file in front of you. I'm a licensed therapist myself. I know how this stuff works. I don't think you've really done much at all in these months to track her down, so I want to know what her name is, and whatever identifying information you have on her in that file so that I can start doing my own search."

Though he was clearly flustered, he nevertheless responded in requisite agency-speak that that wasn't going to be possible, without her consent or a court process, the identifying information was blah blah blah....

I cut him off. "Look it, God wants me to have that information."

There was silence on the phone. Slowly, he replied. "Just so you know, I am an ordained Lutheran minister, so I don't think something like that should be used as an idle threat."

"I'm not making an idle threat at all. I'm telling you, God sent me an angel in a dream and told me what her name was."

Again, a very long stunned silence. "An angel told you her name?"

"Absolutely. My partner and I are going to Italy next week, I want to visit the place where my family is from, and so last week, an angel of the Lord came to me in a dream and told me her name. So, you just open that file and look right there where her name is and I'm going to tell you what her name, as revealed to me by God himself as a sign that He wants me to have this information for my own health and salvation."

He gulped and said, "OK. It's in front of me."

At which point I simply repeated verbatim the message that I had indeed gotten from the angelic voice in the dream. "My mother's name is Gloria."

I remember hearing him give out a kind of shriek and then heard the phone drop and bounce on the floor. Waiting a few moments on my side of the line until he recovered the receiver and his composure, I heard a very different person on the other side of the line when he got back on, and with a voice shaking with something that sounded to me like terror, he managed to speak. "Oh my God, that is her name. Her name is Gloria. Both of your mothers' names are Gloria," at which point, really without even thinking, he simply read off her full name to me, her last known address, and her sister's name who had accompanied her to the hospital.

I thanked him and hung up and took the information that day to the Berkeley Public Library where I got out the phone book for the county in New Jersey where her last known address was located. I called the first person in that phone book with that last name, who ended up being my uncle, my mother's brother, and the very next day, I was speaking on the phone, after 29 years of separation, to my birth mother.

But the story—and the synchronicities—do not end there. One of the more intriguing aspects of my writing career is that my family and friends generally don't read my books. Neither of my Hopcke parents were big readers to start with, and most of my friends haven't been all that interested in the rather academic work in Jungian psychology or Catholic spirituality that has made up the larger part of my work. I know for a fact my own husband Paul—though an academic himself—never read anything I had written. I may be wrong, perhaps some of them have snuck my books into their reading lists, but if they have, they have never told me nor has any of my work sparked any discussion between us. *There Are No Accidents* was a little bit of an exception to this rule, since I interviewed a lot of my friends for the stories that did appear in that book. So, the people whose stories made it into the book read it, that I do know. With regard to my parents, however, while they displayed my books on a bookshelf in their home, they never gave any evidence of ever having read them.

So fast forward eight years to the publication of *Accidents* and one day, out of nowhere, I get a call from my adoptive mother, a little tearful and upset. "I need to ask you something. I was moving books around downstairs and that book you wrote on synchronicity fell out of my hand. So, I picked it up and thought maybe I'd give it a look. So, I just opened it to a random page and read the story of that client of yours who found his birth mother had the same name as his adoptive mother." She struggled to get the words out. "Was that you?"

I was floored. Really what were the odds that my mother, who had never read anything I had written, would by complete chance open my book to the very page where, buried in the middle of a chapter on dreams and synchronicity, in brief and disguised form, I told my own story above? For all kinds of reasons, but chiefly due to her own emotional vulnerability, I had decided not to tell her or my father that I had located my birth mother. Yet, synchronistically, there she was reading the story and intuiting—in a way perhaps only an extraordinarily emotionally sensitive mother could—that the story was about me. What I did know was that on the phone, out of the blue, was certainly no place to disclose this information; I was not ready to do so, nor do I think she was ready to hear it. So, on the spot, I told her an untruth—that the story in *Accidents* she was referring to was indeed about a client (though it wasn't)—and the palpable relief from her response made me think, at the time, that that was the best course of action, But I was left with a lingering ambivalence about whether to disclose to her and my father that I both knew, and was having an ongoing relationship with, my birth mother and that this ambivalence about not telling them continued, literally, until the end of their lives. In the end, whether right or wrong, they died never knowing.

I've gone at some length to tell this story because both the synchronicity of my mothers' names and the subsequent coincidence of the chance discovery of that story in my book provides a good introduction to what I believe is best to begin with: the four aspects of synchronistic events, three of which Jung noted in his work—their acausality, their emotional impact, and their symbolic nature—along with a fourth which subsequent Jungians, including myself, have explored in great depth—their transitional aspect, that is, how such occurrences seem to cluster around times of transition in our lives.

The Unexpected Delights of Acausality

In my talks and classes on synchronicity over the years, I've found it no less true now than when I first began my work in the field 30 years ago that the acausal, random nature of a synchronistic events is at times the most difficult aspect to grasp, hang on to, and affirm. But in the end, it is the very acausal nature of these events which in fact makes them what we call a coincidence. If one wanted to be very concrete and literal with the word, one would be justified in calling just about any two events that happen simultaneously or within close temporal proximity a "coincidence." And yet, that's not what we generally mean by the word. Two events that are linked as cause and effect are *not* what we call a coincidence. If I flip the wall switch and my overhead kitchen light goes on, sure, you could call that a coincidence, since they happened more or less at the same time, but no one would call that a coincidence because I intended to turn the light on and made it happen.

A coincidence is something we *didn't make happen*. Sometimes the random nature of coincidences is striking because the actual probability of the two events occurring together is remote—for example, the one book of many of mine on the shelf falling open to the very story in the middle of a chapter on another topic in front of my mother who had never read anything I had written. I would say the chance of that happening was pretty remote—and yet it did. It was a coincidence. And sometimes the probability of the two events occurring together might be either seen or even statistically proven to be less remote: given my life history and experiences up to the time I contacted the adoption agency, my discovering that I was of Italian background on my mother's side was something that I almost expected.

But the point we need to bear in mind with synchronistic events is actually not how unlikely or likely the probability of the coincidence happens to be, but that, no matter how dramatic or ordinary, *all* coincidences are acausal, that is, not specifically caused or intended or sought. I didn't make *myself* Italian-American. It occurred *to* me, and of course it had a "cause"—my birth mother's ethnic background—but the cumulative coincidence of having no conscious knowledge of my background until relatively late in my life when I discovered, after studying Italian, living in Italy, translating books and tutoring students, that I was *in fact* Italian is what is at the essence of the synchronistic nature of the event.

Beyond the mere coincidental nature of it all is the fact that it was also a *meaningful* coincidence. Chance events co-occur in temporal proximity all the time, and again, concretely, literally, one could say that the fact that it is raining here in northern California on a given day and it is simultaneously raining on the other side of the world in Kathmandu is a coincidence. So is my going down to the corner store in my neighborhood with my dog and, without seeking him out, bumping into my neighbor with his dog. Certainly, a coincidence. But neither co-occurrences have necessarily a great deal of subjective meaning. They are what we call coincidences, but of an everyday, ordinary sort.

Jung coined the term "synchronicity" to denote those coincidences that were not merely ordinary, random events simply co-occurring in time but instead a special category of coincidence: random chance events which were connected, yes, through temporal proximity, but whose real connection lies rather in the *subjective meaningfulness* of the coincidence to the person or persons involved. What makes up the significance of a synchronicity is what I will be discussing shortly, for the meaning of the event is constituted by the three other aspects of synchronistic events that I have mentioned: their emotional impact, their symbolic quality, and their appearance in our lives at times of transition. But first, it's important to emphasize that, first and foremost a psychiatrist, Jung intended synchronicity as a psychological principle of connection, which is what is ensconced in the acknowledgment that it is the *subjective* significance of the events which makes a coincidence a synchronicity.

Put more simply, it isn't the dramatic improbability of the coincidence but that the coincidence *meant* something important to *you*. I do feel the need to reinforce this part of the concept on the basis of years of experience with students and readers who come up to me at talks or write me their stories and conclude by asking me "Is this, that, or the other coincidence a synchronicity?" To which I am always forced to respond, "Only *you* can tell *me* if it is a synchronicity. What did it *mean* to you?" Obviously, if I've been surfing the Internet while writing this book, just happen to click on the Wikipedia article on the city of Zurich where Jung practiced, get a bit curious about the history of the city and glance over the article, and then later flip on Jeopardy only to find out that answer to the final question is "Zurich," well, that's an interesting coincidence, about on par with bumping into a neighbor down the corner, but still, a fairly ordinary coincidence. Obviously, it is a far, far more meaningful coincidence to discover that the message I received in the dream was true, that both my mothers had identical names, and for that specific piece of information to unlock my whole family history to me going back centuries. Now that's a *significant* coincidence, that no one sought or caused.

But let's just say, for the sake of argument, that for some bizarre (not to mention unethical) reason, the social workers at the adoption agency decided to actually pair me with an adoptive mother whom they knew had the same name as my birth mother. In other words, what if the identity of my mothers' shared names was an intentional act they had specifically *caused*? The fact remains that the series of events in *my* life which came together in my story are still an example of synchronicity *to me*, because they were events that I myself in my own subjective experience did not seek out or make happen. Even if intended by social workers back in 1958, the synchronicity of their identical names would be the essence of the meaning to me and the impact on my life in ways that changed it forever. All events have causes; the synchronistic nature of the event lies not out there but instead within us, in what the meaning of the event is to us.

I have found that it is hard for many of us to hang on and affirm the importance, the realness, of our inner life, our unique subjectivity. Our culture is one in which empirical knowledge and the rational, provable science and technology that emerges out of empiricism is highly prized. In this light, I would even go so far as to say that there is in Western culture at large and in American culture especially a prejudice against subjectivity, those immaterial aspects of our lives, the ways and means of our hearts and souls. So, when I talk about syn- chronistic events, which of course are only synchronistic insofar as they are subjectively meaningful to the people involved, listeners or readers (or even my editors and agents, at times) show a level of skepticism or a dismissive attitude toward these stories. "Well, of course it makes sense you are Italian," they'll say after my telling my story—which of course it does, because I am—but *that's not the point*. The resonance of the events in my story lies not in the rational acknowledgement of ethnic heritage but rather in the mysterious way in which everything came to together for me, externally and internally, through a series of random coincidences that I did not cause, and indeed, could not have even anticipated. That is what makes it synchronistic.

So yes, in a way, one could say, from the outside, that the meaningfulness of these events is "made up" by those involved, and that would be true in a sense, insofar as we are talking about subjective meaning. But practically all the greatest achievements of the human culture could likewise be dismissed as "made up:" Beethoven's *Ninth Symphony*, the Empire State Building, *Moby Dick*. None of these are natural phenomena found under a rock somewhere spontaneously evolved into existence on their own. They are all "made up." It is, however, *not* that they are the results of human action but rather that they manifest the subjective vision of the composer, architect and author. It is their subjective meaningfulness to the creator and, by extension, their resonance within us as we hear, encounter or read these "made up" works that is what is important.

Besides, Jung was not so airy-fairy about subjectivity. Rather, he—and we who follow his lead on synchronicity—do not just stop at calling something meaningful simply because someone says it is. One of Jung's great contributions to human knowledge, along with all the other depth psychologists of that era, was the conviction that it is possible to bring a valuable empirical perspective to even subjective phenomena. So, when we experience a coincidence of events as synchronistic, we are indeed saying that it is so because of its subjective meaning *as evidenced by* emotional impact, symbolic power, and transformative effect. Those are what makes a synchronistic event meaningful.

One can well imagine that over the many years of work within this area I have heard hundreds of stories about amazing coincidences. "I was watching my cat walk across the back of the couch, and thought to myself, 'She might fall off if she's not careful,' and right then, as I was thinking it, oh my God, *she did!*" Not to immediately dismiss the possibility that such a coincidence is synchronistic, but if I do, it's not because of the commonality of the occurrence—cats fall off couches and we all bump into neighbors every day—but rather because such a coincidence does not really rise to the level of "meaningful" in the way I've just described, any more than the final Jeopardy answer coinciding with my Wikipedia browsing does. So, what makes up the meaning of a meaningful coincidence?

The Emotional Impact of Our Connections--Synchronistic and Familial

Perhaps the most important psychological aspect of an event's significance speaking lies, quite simply, in its emotional impact. Ordinary coincidences may delight or amuse; synchronistic events resonate deeply and throughout time. Sometimes the confluence of circumstances brings to the surface complex and profound feelings about situations or people that we might only have been dimly aware of, making the unconscious conscious in a distinctive and unavoidable way. Other times the synchronistic occurrence pulls together a constellation of disparate, even conflicting, emotions for us into a single happening; one unitary experience that amplifies or completes an emotional process.

As I have often found the case for myself over the 25 years of writing and researching this topic, synchronicities often happen in the process of my writing and researching, and such was the case with my writing this very section about the emotional aspect of these events. Knowing what I was going to say conceptually, I still needed to give some thought to what sort of a story I had experienced or that people had told me to use here as an illustration. So, having set aside the weekend to think about it, I instead turned my attention last Saturday to my role as an external reader on a doctoral student's dissertation committee at California Institute of Integral Studies in San Francisco, reviewing the somewhat long but very interesting dissertation that was going to be defended later that afternoon.

Though I've served as external reader before at other schools, this was the first time for me on a dissertation committee at CIIS, brought on because the doctoral candidate's topic was on gay Catholic men's experience, and the department needed someone to sit on the committee that had that rather specific expertise. All well and good, and yet, my own history in connection with CIIS has been a long one, because my late husband Paul, who died of early-onset Alzheimer's in January 2013, had taught there for nearly twenty years and had served for a long time as one of the program chairs of their philosophy and religion department. When he began there, though, I was still rather young, at the beginning of my career, and so I was known by his colleagues there as a "faculty spouse." But over the years some of these colleagues of his have grown to become some of my closest friends.

Given all the years of history and connection to the school, my being asked to join a doctoral committee there for the first time, by virtue of my own professional qualifications, was very flattering—mere faculty spouse no more!—and absolutely appropriate to my area of scholarly competency. Yet, as I read through the dissertation and prepared myself to participate in the discussion on its findings that afternoon, I wasn't entirely aware, I'll confess, of the rather bittersweet emotional quality under the surface. It was happening just a couple of weeks after the anniversary of Paul's death in January, which was itself right after the holidays, which to compound the nostalgia and complexity of feelings even further, happens every year just days after what would have been Paul's birthday in mid-November. That day in

January, however, my mind was engaged in intellectual questions of Catholic theology and heuristic research methods, and I had over-looked the emotional experience showing up there would entail. Psychotherapists, even seasoned ones, have their unconscious blind spots.

Well, the moment I arrived, one of my oldest friends who was also on the committee came up to greet me—it was the first time I had seen Connie since her own partner's funeral in the fall, and we had a brief chance to catch up. We were professional, of course, and contained ourselves emotionally enough to talk, but between us, suddenly, I realized, there was the bond of grief, which she had shared when I lost Paul, and I had shared with her when she lost Russell. And then, after bumping into Connie, I had other long-time colleagues of Paul's start to come up to me that day, some of whom I hadn't seen in 20 years, until the whole experience began to be a little disorienting for me, like a reunion: noticing who's aged and how, and who hasn't and why, past and present colliding, as we all catch up with one another all these years later, me now age 57 and no longer in my 20s, and them, with their new professional positions and activities, new families, children and stories. We soon settled down for the formal defense of the dissertation in question—a very moving and artistically inspiring presentation by the doctoral candidate, who was a Franciscan priest. This brought forth yet another connection: my late husband had been in the Franciscan order himself, the two of us had traveled quite a number of memorable times to Assisi together, and the last book we translated together was the collection of medieval folktales about St. Francis entitled *The Little Flowers of St. Francis*, a passage of which I read at his funeral.

After it was all over that day, I drove back along the Pacific coast home with a heart full of much deep feeling—full in a way I hadn't really been prepared for, to tell the truth—and even on the way home, I confess I wasn't entirely aware of exactly what I was feeling, until I stopped in San Francisco midway home to get some gas. And there, while leaning up against the car, putting gas in the gas tank, I heard my phone chime with a text from a friend with whom I hadn't spoken in many months, sending me, of all things, out of nowhere, a picture of someone who bore an uncanny resemblance to my Paul, particularly as he looked 25 years ago, when he taught at CIIS, with the text "OMG, doesn't this look like Paul." My response there at the gas station was strong and immediate after the day I had spent, and I thought, "It does. But it's not." And with that, all my grief—grief of many months, grief of that afternoon—came flooding up, and I took some time there before driving on to have a good, solid, thorough cry. I missed him.

"Uncanny" is often the word that is used for the ruthless appropriateness of a synchronistic event's emotional impact, and later in this book, I'll delve more fully into this term, but for now, it's enough to say that receiving this text with this picture felt especially uncanny: to have my whole afternoon engaged, for the first time in my own right, at my late husband's school, with so many reminders and associations to him, literal, symbolic, social and professional; to share my grief mutually with Connie who was, herself, grieving the loss of her partner; and then to have Paul's relationship, our relationship, to the life and spirit of St. Francis, brought forward by the presentation itself, only to have a friend I hadn't heard from in such a long time text me such an evocative picture at the one moment I wasn't driving: it all come together for me emotionally, who he was--and who he wasn't—now in my life without him.

Through my tears there in the car at the Shell Station on 6th Street, I realized the entirety of what I was feeling as a widower, that difficult and ambivalent connection I have—that all of us who have lost spouses have—to those who are gone and yet who are, in so many ways, not gone. Our lives have the shape they do without them because of them. We are who we are because of our marriage to them and the lives we shared. And I realized it there because of a perfectly timed, synchronistically delivered text, in the very middle of my reflecting upon what sort of illustration I would use for the emotional impact discussion here.

For all my experience as a therapist and in my own therapy over the years, I'm not shy about admitting that that afternoon I was blindsided by the depth of grief that got unlocked. As these things do, it looks so obvious when written on paper and viewed in retrospect. But Jung definitely would have understood, for he held the view that far from being surprised at our unconsciousness, we should rather, individually and collectively, be much more surprised at our *consciousness*. Consciousness, he thought, is a much more miraculous and fragile state, only attained with great difficulty and in spite of much resistance, and easily lost. *Un*consciousness was the more common human state, in his view—born without awareness into this life and only very slowly over the course of our development coming into very fragmentary flickers of knowing who we are.

In writing about Eastern spiritual practices, he put it somewhat poetically:

> Consciousness does not create itself—it wells up from unknown depths. In childhood it awakens gradually, and all through life it wakes each morning out of the depths of sleep from an unconscious condition. It is like a child that is born daily out of the primordial womb of the un-conscious. . . . It is not only influenced by the unconscious but continually emerges out of it in the form of numberless spontaneous ideas and sudden flashes of thought. ["The Psychology of Eastern Meditation," *CW 11*, par. 935.]

As I often say, there's actually nothing in my daily life or experience that contradicts Jung's view. We spend literally a third of our lives in actual unconsciousness, sleeping. Even in our so-called "waking lives," I see most of us walking around in a relative state of unconsciousness throughout our day—if not in an actual fog of self-absorption (usually the people driving in front of us or sitting in the middle of the aisle at the grocery store or standing in the middle of the sidewalk on their smart phones as we are trying to get somewhere), then often simply on "auto-pilot," doing and saying things out of force of custom or habit until later we ask, "Where did I put my keys?" or "Did I actually forget to run the dishwasher?" Indeed, a sustained experience of concentrated consciousness requires a special operation for most people—meditation, prayer, some kind of psychological discipline—and generally that, too, is neither easy, quick or especially long-lasting.

So, the emotional impact of synchronistic effects arises largely out of this base state of unawareness that tends to be characteristic of how we live our imperfect human lives, especially in a culture that prizes production and efficiency and doesn't generally make much space for feeling or feeling experience. Feelings are messy, irrational, inconvenient, we are told. Feelings are best contained, directed, and used, we are encouraged to think. And so, if we get into the habit of pushing them aside, noticing but not delving in, letting them have some space over here on the fringe of awareness while we go about doing what we need to do—which is certainly what I myself had done around my grief that holiday season—then the confluence of events which makes them suddenly, powerfully, unavoidably conscious—felt in their fullness, rich in their depth and variety—takes on the character of a meaningful coincidence.

The uncanniness of these coincidences, though, displays not just the general emotional meaningfulness of a synchronicity—their "feelingfulness"—but, more particularly to the topic of this book, the special quality of relationship that we call "family." These synchronicities are meaningful, because they occur within relationships that have a special emotional power for us. It was my husband I was grieving, the man I had spent my life with—not a neighbor or a distance professional acquaintance who had died—and I shared that grief with

Connie who was also grieving her beloved life partner. I'm tempted to say that "family" itself is a kind of acausal connecting principle: the relationships that constitute our family connections, though sometimes originally grounded in choices of spouse or intentional adoptions or other voluntary associations, nevertheless take on a special complexity of connection over time and with lived, shared history that places them in a category of relationship that is like no other.

Jung had many, many experiences of synchronicities within the ambit of his family connections that he tells us about in his auto-biography, *Memories, Dreams, Reflections*:

> The unconscious helps by communicating things to us, or making figurative allusions. It has other ways, too, of informing us of things which by all logic we could not possible know. Consider synchronistic phenomena, pre-monitions, and dreams that come true. I recall one time during the Second World War when I was returning home from Bollingen. I had a book with me, but could not read, for the moment the train started to move, I was over-powered by the image of someone drowning. This was a memory of an accident that had happened while I was on military service. During the entire journey I could not rid myself of it. It struck me as uncanny, and I thought, "What has happened? Can there have been an accident?"
>
> I got out at Erlenbach and walked home, still troubled by this memory. My second daughter's children were in the garden. The family was living with us, having returned to Switzerland from Paris because of the war. The children stood looking rather upset, and when I asked, "Why, what is the matter?" they told me that Adrian, then the youngest of the boys, had fallen into the water in the boathouse. It is quite deep there, and since he could not really swim he had

almost drowned. His older brother had fished him out. This had taken place at exactly the time I had been assailed by that memory in the train. The unconscious had given me a hint. Why should it not be able to inform me of other things also?

Frequently foreknowledge is there, but not recognition. Thus I once had a dream in which I was attending a garden party, I saw my sister there, and that greatly surprised me, for she had died some years before. A deceased friend of mine was also present. The rest were people who were still alive. Presently I saw that my sister was accompanied by a lady I knew well. Even in the dream I had drawn the conclusion that the lady was going to die. "She is already marked," I thought. In the dream I knew exactly who she was. I knew also that she lived in Basel. But as soon as I woke up I could no longer, with the best will in the world, recall who she was, although the whole dream was still vivid in my mind. I pictured all my acquaintances in Basel to see whether the memory images would ring a bell. Nothing. A few weeks later I received news that a friend of mine had had a fatal accident. I knew at once that she was the person I had seen in the dream but had been unable to identify. My recollection of her was perfectly clear and richly detailed. . . . (*MDR*, pp. 302-303)

Premonitory synchronicities such as Jung's tempt us to adduce explanations of hidden causes to make sense of them, but I believe this is because we find ourselves a bit scared around the power of the unconscious and the depth of feeling that our family connections evoke. I'd like to call the reader's attention to the way in which Jung himself, in telling these stories of his grandson's near death, his wife's cousin's passing, and his sister's dreamtime accompaniment of an acquaintance soon to leave this life, doesn't try to explain why he had these synchronistic experiences. He doesn't even go into what they "meant." Their meaningfulness, in a way, is self-evident; of course, his unconscious emotional attachment to his grandson, wife's family, and deceased sister is strong, vivid, and significant. Psychologically, that is the most important aspect of these stories.

Even if we were to posit that Jung was endowed with some verifiable "sixth sense," an actual clairvoyant ability that enabled him to experience events psychically while they were happening elsewhere or envision the future through predictive dreams, the events he narrates here would still be synchronistic in the psychological sense because our family relationships are an especially potent locus of our emotional experience in this life. "Explaining" them as psychic phenomena still leaves their psychological significance to the individual involved to be appreciated. The uncanniness of them and why that depth of feeling is constellated has to do, in large part, with the nature of the relationships within which they occurred—the most important relationships in Jung's life, and in ours—our families. And because this relational matrix is for most of us a given, we are to a large degree throughout our ordinary lives unconscious of its power over us—so familiar, to use an apt word—that we don't see it, feel it, or appreciate it until external events come together so weirdly, so perfectly as to make the profundity of familial connections a conscious and vivid emotional reality again.

A Symbolic Life

The second feature of the meaningfulness of a synchronistic event is, I have noticed, that such coincidences often cluster or occur around a particular, specific symbol or set of symbols in our lives, and which, with an eye toward our topic here, have a specific power or meaning in the stories of our families. Indeed, these images or objects or situations are very frequently at the very center of the synchronicity. Two such examples that come to my mind immediately, and that serve as illustrations of this symbolic quality, are from stories told to me by a pair of different clients.

The first, Jan, had come into psychotherapy with me for a number of different issues, one of which definitely was the uncertainty and stress caused by her vocation as a professional musician, a difficult way to support oneself for all kinds of reasons. Like most professional musicians, she told me, she made her regular living teaching music in a local private school and through private lessons, but she said her performance career was "so-so," partly because of and partly in spite of her instrument—the double bassoon. Because it was an unusual instrument to play, she told me that she found herself in demand, but for the same reason, the demand for her expertise was variable. "Not every ensemble needs a contrabassoon but I'm lucky in the sense that, if they do, I'm one of the first people they think of."

As we will be exploring more fully in the next section, I've learned over the many years of my work that people often come into psychotherapy at a time of transition in their lives. Sometimes that transition is explicit and acknowledged—a breakup, a death in the family—but often the transition people need to make is something they are resisting or afraid of admitting. So, as I listened over a number of months to Jan describe the vagaries, the disappointments, the frustrations of her persisting in a performance career, it was during a session after yet another "thanks, but no thanks" audition experience she had had, when yet again she didn't get the job, that I took it upon myself to wonder aloud if she had considered alternative performance opportunities, maybe a different instrument, a different repertoire, perhaps...

In an uncharacteristically quick and forceful way, she sat up in the chair in response to my opening that door of exploration with her and quite firmly said to me, "I know playing the contrabassoon is what I'm meant to do."

Which is when I finally heard the full story.

"I feel very fortunate in a lot of ways about my upbringing. Though I grew up on the East Coast, both my parents were from the Midwest where their families had deep roots going back to the 1800s. So, both my parents were very stable, practical, salt-of-the-earth kind of people, with lots of common sense, and both me and my sister were the focus of their complete attention. Again, very family-oriented, almost to a fault, I would say, and as I we grew up, she and I began to understand a little bit of the background as to why they were that way with us, as we learned that neither of them had come, themselves, from very stable families. My mother's parents were rather advanced in years when she was born an only child, so she was at a relatively early age in her life when they both passed on, more or less at the same time she met my father, right after high school. And my father's background, I will say, almost constituted a kind of family mystery for us. I remember my sister or me asking about our grandparents, his parents, now and then, you know, in response to some kind of school assignment about genealogy or maybe because we had gone out with the grandparents of some of our friends, and in his typical, polite way, he would say these very vague things about them—you know, like 'that's a long story, Jan,' or 'hmm, one of these days when you are older, we'll sit down, and I'll tell you all about it'—or if we had caught him in a bad mood, we'd even get a sharp response, 'I really don't want to talk about it' or 'I don't know what's happening with them.' Obviously, putting two and two together, it became clear that for reasons unknown my father was pretty distinctly estranged from his father—my grandmother had died when I was little—and furthermore, it was also clear that my father did not appreciate its being brought up as a topic of conversation.

"Because of the sort of people they were, you can imagine, they were very ambivalent about my pursuing a musical career, for all the reasons normal protective parents are, but in their case perhaps a little more so. I know absolutely that they would have preferred that I majored in something with more promise of a stable, income-producing career. My mother consistently pushed library sciences on me, and my father, ever the engineer, repeatedly, 'suggested' that I explore something science or technology-oriented, though I had never shown any interest or aptitude in anything of the sort. But from an early age, I was the artistic one, loved performing, dancing, singing, being in front of people. I took up an instrument in elementary school--first the clarinet, then in junior high school, the various saxophones because the school band needed a fuller section. The assistant band leader was trying to put together a small chamber-style orchestra, and he himself played the bassoon, so that was how I made my way to the bassoon and then eventually, under his tutelage, to the contrabassoon, which he specifically introduced to me so that he and I could round out the winds on certain pieces the ensemble would perform. So, at first, it was really his idea that I play the contrabassoon, but for reasons I can't really explain, I immediately felt like this particular, rather unusual instrument was 'right' for me.

"Even though all my teachers and conductors made it very clear I had a special gift for this instrument and I myself loved it, as time went on, you can't help but second-guess yourself when it comes to something as uncertain as an artistic or musical calling, especially without enthusiastic parental support. Once finished college (where, again, due to my parents' diffidence, I had only minored in music, rather than majoring in it, as I might have wished), I was at a point where I was realizing just how hard the path forward as a performer would be. The gigs were few and far between, especially for such a specialized instrument. Then there was a certain level of sexism I was encountering on top of all the regular challenges. And both my parents, but especially my dad, made it amply clear that I would be on my own after my undergraduate degree if professional music was what I was determined to pursue. I wouldn't say that this particular boundary they drew caused a rift between us—I didn't really expect them to support me after I graduated, nor was it something I especially wanted either at that age, quite eager to be independent and less beholden to them—but it was a definite point of punctuation in our relationship, especially given how unconditionally supportive and loving they had been throughout my childhood. My decision to go into music, though it was mine and taken with full cognizance and of my own volition, nevertheless did feel like a door had closed behind me, and they had closed it.

"We maintained contact, of course, and in fact, on the surface everything between us seemed to go on as it always had, very cordial and warm, holidays at home, and so on. But there had definitely been a shift in the emotional tone of my relationship with them, and I began to see that side of my father which I guess I would call 'hard,' stubborn, grudging, closed down. And over time with my own maturity, this side of him then began to make a little more emotional sense of the family mystery—the complete estrangement that had existed my whole life between him and his father. None of this, however, kept me from following my dream and I got myself into a master's program in music—as much as to credential myself for an income-producing job as a teacher as to finally begin to dedicate myself to what I had long felt was my true vocation. But I won't lie, I continued to harbor some serious doubts about whether or not I was deluding myself around a musical career.

"I was in grad school when we got word that my grandfather, my father's father, died. I was little surprised at the news, which came to me in a pretty terse phone call from my dad one evening, and during that short conversation, I got more information about my grandfather in that half hour than I think my sister and I had ever heard in all the previous years put together. Evidently, my father explained, he had been in a nursing home for some time, which had followed upon quite a number of rehab facilities and group home situations for what my father simply called his 'drinking.' I remember that particular 'aha' moment quite vividly. As a matter of fact, when suddenly I got the missing piece of the puzzle, that made sense of the whole pattern, and with the topic at last opened by my grandfather's passing, I was able to at last have that long-delayed conversation with my dad who talked about his father's alcoholism, the instability it created, the sense of being on his own, and finally his own decision to stop taking care of him. Behind the scenes, he told me, he and my mother would occasionally get word, either from him or from various personnel at the facilities he was checking into, about my grandfather's condition, the state of his recovery—which was never very long term—and his desire to reconcile, all of which my father, consistently, resolutely, received, and did not respond to.

"But now he was gone, and the house my father had grown up in—which my grandfather had vacated for quite some time—needed to be closed up and sold off. So, my sister and I both went with him out to Iowa that summer—curious as all get out, of course, about what we would find, now that the seal of silence had been lifted from this whole section of our family history. But I will also say, given the low, simmering tension between my dad and me, there was also a sense that this car trip out to my father's hometown in the middle of Iowa marked a little bit of a shift for the better between us. Maybe because my grandfather's passing freed my father, freed him from the burden of the painful conflicts my grandfather's drinking had caused, freed him from the need to hold him away, freed him to take this trip back to his own past, his own childhood, his own roots.

"It was a big old rambling Victorian home, hard to believe one little old man had been living in it all by himself before being placed in skilled nursing. My dad had already made arrangements for the local estate sellers to come through and empty the place in a week or two, but, for all his protestations that he could care less what happened to everything, the fact was that he did want to go through it first and make sure he took whatever mementos or other objects of largely sentimental value from his childhood he still wanted—once again, a softer side to my father peeked through, and it wasn't lost on either my sister or on me.

"Anyway, as my father took his time on the first floor, where all the old-timey 1930s and 1940s furniture was still in place in the parlor, dining room and quiet, sunny sitting room, my sister and I head up to the attic. As I said, it was summertime, so I do remember expecting it to be pretty hot, but I guess the place was well-insulated because it was actually quite cool and pleasant, a couple of large triangular gable windows letting in a fair bit of light. My sister takes one end of the attic and I take the other, and as I'm going through the various boxes and things up there, really not seeing much of any real worth or interest when suddenly in the back corner, I see this instrument case which, when I open it, I'm stunned to find, has a double bassoon in it! Absolutely, positively the last thing I would have expected to find up here—the very instrument I play?

"That was the goosebumps moment. Completely weird. I examine the case and sure enough, there's a name inscribed on a small silver plaque on the case which is not my grandfather's and which I do not recognize, and right away I can tell that this instrument is pretty darn old, but getting there, probably from the same era as the rest of the house and its furnishing, early 20th century. I take it out and check out what kind of condition it's in, and it seems like you could play it if you really wanted to spend some money to restore it, so not some priceless antique instrument in perfect condition, not at all, but still, a contrabassoon in the attic of my grandfather whom I never knew and never met.

"Obviously, at that point I take it downstairs and say, 'Hey, dad, look at this,' and he is about as surprised and mystified as I am, and he is looking at it with his perfect 'what the heck' expression on.

"I point to the name on the plaque. 'Do you know who that is?' Which is when my dad starts to laugh, and puts his hand on mine.

"'Oh my God, honey, that is so strange. I never knew that.' He looked up at me. 'That's your great-great-grandfather. My father's mother's father, his grandfather.'

"Since my dad had, throughout my life, closed the door on his own past to us, it occurred to me then that I didn't even know my own family's names, which created a bit of a poignant moment between the two of us then, like my father realized how much he had been holding back, from himself and from us. But there I am, literally, physically holding this old double-bassoon that had belonged to my great-great-grandfather, at which point, I seize the moment, look my dad straight in the eye, after all the years between the two of us spent wrangling oh so politely about my own musical career playing the double bassoon, and say in exactly the tone of voice he liked to use with me—firm, forceful, no-nonsense: 'So what you are saying is that my great-great-grandfather appears to have *also* been a double bassoonist.' That *also* was probably the largest, loudest, heaviest *also* ever spoken between two people.

"Was he sheepish? Apologetic? Bewildered? All of the above? All my father could manage to say in response was 'I guess so, honey. I guess he must have been.' For me, I will say, it was not just the most unlikely of coincidences, but right then and there, a moment of vindication for me, because as it turns out, evidently, from what we could figure out, my great-great-grandfather had been a professional double-bassoonist, since when all three of us then went back up into the attic, we found nearby a box full of music with his name on the scores, double-bassoon parts for various works that were clearly marked up for actual performance, a couple of lesson books likewise with handwritten notes, and a number of different manuscripts with original solo parts, which looked like cadenzas that he had come up with on his own. My father spent the rest of that morning, from what I could tell, in a state of gentle wonder, which was gratifying for both my sister and me. It was like the discovery of this hidden connection between his daughter and his own great-grandfather somehow put his own painful relationship between his father and himself into a larger context, made it seem like a smaller part of a larger and more important history. Or maybe that's just what I was reading into it. But I can say that the import of this coincidence was not lost on my father, and from that point onward, the whole emotional tenor of our trip changed from a kind of resentful annoyance for him to something almost tender and wistful. And not just the tenor of that trip at the time but ever after, because, though he might not have ever been able to articulate it, never again did he ever take a hard line or oppositional tone with me about my playing.

"Obviously, I took the instrument and the music with me, and I still have it. It doesn't make any sense to have that particular instrument restored, the one I have is more modern and I'm used to it, but still— what are the chances of that? My great-great-grandfather was *also* a double bassoonist. Especially given that instrument. It's not like he played the piano or the violin, something common. And it has been more than once when my parents have come over to my place and seen the instrument that my father has said to me, 'You know, I really do wish now that I had taken the chance I had to get more information about this while he was alive.' Which I think is about as direct an admission of regret I will ever hear from him about his own estrangement from his father and an apology from him to me about his own hard-headedness around my vocation."

A second similar story about discovering a specific symbol with a family meaning comes from my client, Frank, who confessed to having a bit of a "pelican" thing. For all kinds of reasons, people often find themselves having a specific affinity for a particular animal or animals. Sometimes these "spirit animals" are part of an explicit family tradition, as among native peoples or tribes. Sometimes there's just a certain aesthetic attraction to, say, horses or dogs. Other times, as in Frank's case, it can be traced to a childhood experience.

"My favorite uncle went to Disneyland once, which for me as a little kid, had a very magical and mystical aura about it and he bought me a little stuffed pelican there and brought it back to me as a souvenir, which for me then was like he had visited another planet and brought me back this amazing object from some far-off heaven realm. I loved that pelican, and soon as a kid, I began collecting other little stuffed pelicans, pelican labels and stickers, there was a local gas station that used a pelican as its mascot, so to speak, so I have a bunch of their advertising and merchandising. Occasionally, people would give me stork objects and I remember as a child getting very exasperated at their confusing pelicans and storks—*not the same thing!* Anyway, I'd say I eventually grew somewhat out of the more obsessive childhood phase of it, but as an adult, it's kind of a little idiosyncratic piece of me. For example, I have a little pelican keychain, and in fact, I still have that pelican my uncle brought me, sitting up on a bookshelf in my office.

"Anyway, thanks to Ancestry.com, my wife began to research her family history, which got me a little curious about mine. I knew my family had emigrated sometime in the 1800s from the old Austro-Hungarian Empire, and my dad seemed to think they had been some kind of aristocrat or minor nobility back then, that was the family mythology at the time. So, in the course of my tracing us back, I not only spent some time up the hill at the Mormon Temple in front of their computers with a very kind volunteer helping me put together the family tree, but my dad had a couple of old great-aunts he hadn't spoken to in a long a while whom he managed to contact. As it turned out, one of them, who was at this point in her late 90s, had a lot of information about the family—she had actually kept a whole series of scrapbooks with family trees and charts, photographs of relatives, some of which were almost 100 years old, just all kinds of material. And, in the course of our talking to her on the phone one night, she said, 'And you do know that our side of the family was actually endowed with a family crest?'

"My father and I both shook our heads. 'Uh, no.'

"'Oh yes, she said, our family provided service to the emperor back in the mid-1600s in recognition of which our family was titled and given a family crest. I have it upstairs somewhere in a closet. You never saw it?'

"My father laughed. 'When and why would I have seen it?' So, a couple of weeks later, God bless her heart, she got one of my dad's second cousins out near her there to box up a bunch of this stuff and send it to us, and as we pulled out the various scrapbooks and papers and photographs, my father burst out laughing.

"'Well, there you go!' he said, and there was our family crest—with a pelican right in the middle of it! As she had said, there was a little write-up about the circumstances of the family's history around its entitlement but also a little description of the meaning of the heraldic crest with a bunch of verbiage I didn't really understand about the colors and the positions, etc. But about the pelican in the middle, it was written that the bird was a symbol of self-sacrifice and so held a prominent place in our family's coat of arms due to the service my ancestors had rendered and the blood the family had spilled for the good of the empire. I've subsequently read that the mythology of the pelican was that mother pelicans were thought to wound themselves in order to nourish their young with their own blood, and since my family's name is etymologically related, as it happens, to the old German word for blood, this set of symbolisms around pelicans totally fit together. It very well may have influenced the original choice of the heraldic symbol.

"For me, though, what was, of course, entirely unexpected and completely synchronistic was the absolutely spontaneous way in which the symbolism of his bird had been a part of my own life since when I was child—only to have it confirmed much, much later by discovering my family's ancestral heraldic symbol was, in fact, the pelican."

Depending on one's point of view and one's academic discipline, one can define what a symbol is in a wide variety of ways. Jung used a fairly succinct definition which could be easily understood and applied to our psychological or emotional experience. A symbol is, in the psychological sense, the best possible expression for something that is not and cannot ever be fully known. "Every psychological expression is a symbol if we assume that it states or signifies something more and other than itself which eludes our present knowledge." ["Definitions," *CW* 6, par. 817.] So, while aspects of a symbol's meaning—what it points to, what it expresses about the unknown—can be illuminated or explored, ultimately, the totality of a symbol's meaning, in Jung's view, cannot ever be fully known or, therefore, exhausted.

For this reason, Jung distinguished between a symbol and a sign. Insignia on uniforms, for instance, are not symbols but signs that identify the wearer. A sign indicates one thing and one thing only. However, in dealing with unconscious material (dreams, fantasies, etc.), the images can be interpreted as symptomatic signs pointing to known or knowable facts, or symbolically, as expressing something essentially unknown. For example,

> the interpretation of the cross as a symbol of divine love is semiotic [i.e., as a mere sign], because "divine love" describes the fact to be expressed better and more aptly than a cross, which can have many other meanings. On the other hand, an interpretation of the cross is *symbolic* when it puts the cross beyond all conceivable explanations, regarding it as expressing an as yet unknown and incomprehensible fact of a mystical or transcendent, i.e., psychological, nature, which simply finds itself most appropriately represented in the cross. ["Definitions," *CW* 6, par. 815.]

Therefore, whether something—an image, a situation, a word, a number—is interpreted as a symbol—pointing to something greater than itself and ultimately not fully knowable or explainable—or as a sign—the image means this, that word means *only* that—depends mainly on the attitude of the observer.

However, in the course of his long experience as a psychotherapist, with which my own experience completely accords, Jung felt that one of the essential characteristics of human beings, one of our special gifts as a species, was our capacity for symbolic thought. Human beings create and use signs to communicate but we are also endowed with the capacity to create and use symbols in order to enlarge and enrich our experience of ourselves, to reach toward the transcendent, to express and share the mysteries of our existence with others. As he put it, "Psychic development cannot be accomplished by intention and will alone; it needs the attraction of the symbol, whose value quantum exceeds that of the cause." ["On Psychic Energy," *CW 8*, par. 47.]

Thus, in his work as a healer, Jung did all he could to foster and encourage what he called a "symbolic attitude," which I believe needs to lead the practice of what I have come to call "symbolic living." This symbolic attitude toward life that Jung tried to foster in his patients should, ideally, I believe, result in going about one's daily life giving priority to understanding the meaning or purpose of psychological phenomena, rather than seeking a reductive explanation. For that reason, I tend to counter people's temptation to resort to a reductive explanation, rather than a symbolic and constructive attitude. Frequently, habitually, when, in the course of discussing synchronistic events, a patient or a reader will tell me about incidents such as Jan's or Frank's and then end by asking me "What's a double-bassoon mean?" or "What did that pelican image mean?" My only response is and can be, "I don't know. Let's work with it." A symbol's meaning cannot ever be fully known but aspects of what it expresses can be brought forward to be appreciated and perhaps integrated.

Indeed, Jung's primary interest in symbols lay in their ability to transform and redirect instinctive energy. "In abstract form, symbols are religious ideas; in the form of action, they are rites or ceremonies. They are the manifestation and expression of excess libido. At the same time, they are stepping-stones to new activities...." ["On Psychic Energy," *CW 8*, par. 91.]

We shouldn't be surprised at all, then, that in synchronistic events the symbol-making nature of our psyches takes center stage, and in these cases, at least part of the mysterious meaning of the symbols in these uncanny coincidences with our forebears definitely lay in the confirmatory quality of the symbols in question. Uncertain of her own call to a musical career, Jan discovered in the symbolic connection to her ancestor through the specific instrument they both shared a more solid sense of the rightness of what she was doing, that, in a way, it— and she, therefore—had a place in the sweep of her family's history. Likewise with Frank, who realized in ways that cannot be explained causally, his idiosyncratic interest in pelican imagery held a larger familial and ancestral meaning. Indeed, the discovery of the coat of arms not only enlarged his conscious knowledge about his family-- which would have been synchronistic enough on its own—but the actual symbolic meanings of the pelican, the qualities of self-sacrificing parenthood and the particular imagery of blood, as related to his family's name, widened Frank's psychological and emotional world and sense of self. It transformed the raw energy of his interest into stepping stone into a broader and deeper consciousness of himself, and it did so through the context of his family connections.

Transitions—Stepping Back to Move Forward More Securely

Beyond their emotional impact and their symbolic nature, the third aspect of the meaningfulness of a synchronistic event is one which Jung himself did not explicitly describe but which I have come to see as an essential part of such an experience, namely, their transitional quality. Such coincidences always occur for people during times of transition; sometimes those transitions are inward—changes in emotional states, attitudes or outlook on life—and sometimes those transitions are outward—changes in relationship, career, jobs, birth and death. Sometimes those transitions are part of a conscious process, as when a synchronistic event occurs in the course of, say, looking for a new job or trying to put new life into one's social or romantic life.

In *There Are No Accidents*, I recounted many of the stories of how strange and wholly unexpected coincidences led to people, who knew they needed to leave their partners or their jobs, being suddenly surprised when opportunities presented themselves in unanticipated ways to move that process along in a direction they hadn't intended or even imagined. But equally intriguing, if not delightful, for me, as a psychotherapist interested in the ways and means of our unconscious lives is how many times a synchronistic event will bring to our attention a transition that we are in the midst of making without consciously knowing it. And because the synchronistic event brings this unconscious transition to consciousness abruptly for us, often it is experienced, initially at least, as unwelcome, decidedly *not* what we wanted.

As my friend Carol tells her story, "How I met my second husband Lloyd is very synchronistic, because I met him 30 years before I actually *met* him—and under the same circumstances 30 years later.

"So, when I first moved to California 30 years ago for nursing school, before I even met my first husband Dan, I was on BART, the Bay Area subway system, from where I lived in Oakland on my way to class over at San Francisco State. I grew up in a family of knitters, sewers and crafters, so there was never a time in my life when I haven't been working on some kind of knitting, crocheting or quilting project, and as is usually the case, more than one simultaneously. That day I remember quite vividly because I was rolling a hank of yarn into a ball, one of 40 such skeins of yarn I would need to ball for a beautiful red woolen afghan that I still have today in my guest room. So, there I am, with the yarn draped over my knees, doing the best I can in the BART train, when a somewhat older gentleman boards and sits in the seat opposite me. I say older because at that time I was in my early 20s, and he was definitely then in his 40s. Of course, the train is stop and go, and being that he's facing me, he can't help see what I'm doing, so eventually he very sweetly strikes up a conversation about my knitting, telling me that seeing me winding the yarn reminds him of his mother and how as a child, she used to have him help her do the winding by making him hold the yarn between his hands for her.

"I hear he has a bit of an English accent and, being somewhat of the young flirt that I was at the time, single, female student-nurse, I laughed and said he should be my guest and had him hold out his hands, over which I then draped the hank of yarn. It was a little strange, I suppose, for the middle of a commuter train, but it was the San Francisco Bay Area, and we're known around here for being pretty free-spirited, not to mention since then I can tell you I have seen much, much stranger things going on in public transit than a couple of complete strangers who just met winding yarn. In short, it was one of those delightful chance encounters, during which I learned his name, Lloyd, that he was a professor at Cal in the art department, and, indeed, as was obvious, he was originally from England, actually the north of England. He told me he still had family back there and had a house there, so he always went back there for the summer. I don't seem to recall disclosing much about myself to him—I really don't know much I would have disclosed since I was young and not a whole lot had happened to me at that point in my life, moving out the Bay Area was really my first big life adventure—but I do remember his story, he was charming of course in that polite British way, inspiring visions of Daphne DuMaurier and Henry James, with a cultured English family, houses by the sea, expatriate professor, and so on. And naturally, a little bit of what happens while you are knitting or crocheting a project gets somewhat woven up into the piece for you while you are working on it, which meant that now and then I would remember the BART ride in which the debonair English professor helped me wind the yarn. Needless to say, we never crossed paths again.

"Meanwhile, I live my life, get my nursing degree, go to work, and eventually meet my husband Dan, get married, we have our kids, I put my work life on hold to raise the kids, and all in all, our family is happy—or so I think. Eventually, I find out, not so much for Dan, and without going into all the gory details about it all here, through a series of slips on his part and an eventually confession, Dan tells me that he has been having an ongoing relationship with someone he works with for a number of years. To be brief about it, we unsuccessfully try to work it out with one another, but it's clear there's no saving the marriage, so we move forward, get our divorce, after which he goes on to marry and begin a second family with this other woman.

"I probably don't need to make clear how all of this was very, very unexpected and very, very painful for me. This was not the life or family I wanted, nor was it the life I thought I had. So, I'll admit, the process of really coming to grips with what had happened to my marriage took quite a long time for me, and it was especially hard, looking at the way I had been so unconscious about the distance that had grown up between us. Angry, guilty, sorry for myself—I felt it all. I'm telling this story in the context of life transitions, and well, to be honest, this transition, which is the nicest way to put it, really, was absolutely, hands-down the hardest I've had to face in my life.

"Not unsurprisingly, as I knew from some of my friends' lives post-divorce, the change in my financial circumstances—with three kids still in school and an ex-husband with a relatively modest income of his own—meant that now in my late 40s, I was going to have to go back to work full-time. I can't say that that was precisely a tragedy, since I had always enjoyed nursing, and my ex and I had planned for me returning to work once the kids would come to college age anyway. Plus, I'm fortunate that the nursing profession is such that I could retool and enter back into the workforce without too much problem. But weirdly, that's actually how I found myself back on BART, 30 years later, with a knitting project in my bag, on my way to a class I needed to take at SF City College for my nursing re-certification, and almost like a déjà vu, a rather nice-looking older gentleman sat down next to me.

"In between my rows of knitting, I could see him scrolling through pictures on his iPhone, when one of them happened to catch my eye—a super cute picture of a dog—so I made a comment, and we struck up a conversation, in the course of which it slowly becomes clear to me, mostly by his British accent and the fact that he had gotten on BART at the downtown Berkeley station, that this is Lloyd, the very same art professor from Cal that almost 30 years ago that helped me wind my yarn on BART for the cardinal-red crocheted afghan I still have!

"At first, I'm pretty dumb-founded. You know, it seems like a very weird set of parallel circumstances. I've only met this guy now twice in my whole life, both times on BART, both times on my way to class for nursing, both times knitting, both times single. When I tell him that in fact we have met before, 30 years before, right here on BART, I think he thought I was a little crazy because he had absolutely NO recollection of our first meeting, the yarn-winding, nothing. But I tell him that we had a whole delightful encounter that had stuck in my mind as part of the afghan project I had been working on, he was a Cal professor, had a house in England where he spent the summers, etc., and in fact I even knew his name, Lloyd. At which point he started laughing, 'Either you are a very persistent stalker or have a superb memory.'

"The oddness of the parallels struck me as a bit of a sign, and I'm not someone who goes about looking for signs in life, to tell you the truth, but of course, in contrast to the first time we met, I had lived a whole lifetime since, and so, I was a lot more self-disclosive this time, appropriately so, given I'm a grown woman now and not just a kid. Likewise, Lloyd—I learned his own wife had died some years before, he was coming to the end of his own teaching career, and so was in somewhat of a life transition of his own, 'bit at a loose end,' as he would put it. We exchanged phone numbers before I got off, he texted me the next day to see if I was free for coffee and that is actually how the two of us started dating."

Carol's story exemplifies a number of the different strands which make up the transitional quality of synchronistic events—it's not just a story of how the coincidence marks a specific *external* transition—from the end of her marriage into the beginning of her next relationship— but also the particularly apt timing of her meeting Lloyd the second time marks the way in which this potential new relationship grows out of her having finally made a successful *internal* emotional transition through and out of her last relationship. So often such synchronistic events almost feel like they didn't or maybe even couldn't have happened until that special time when at last we were ready for them.

In talking with her, she said, "I do wonder sometimes how it would have been had I met Lloyd again, say, one year earlier, when I was really in the depths of my depression and very, very closed down. I don't know if I would have even realized he was sitting next to me in BART. There were times during that period when I found it hard to talk to my own children, no less a stranger on a train."

The intersection of external and internal transition that appears within synchronistic events, however, has its sibling in the intersection of conscious and unconscious transition which, likewise, makes up the core of a synchronistic experience for us as well. Carol was very conscious, of course, of the quite momentous transition she and her family were in the middle of during that period—indeed, the very reason she was on the train going to work again regularly was her divorce—but what the coincidence of meeting Lloyd again in the same circumstances 30 years later brought immediately to her attention— and one can read this some in how she talks about the effect of it on her—was how she was now ready to explore another relationship. She was making a transition back into life, back into love, forward into the future, in a way that at the time she herself wasn't fully aware of—until the second meeting with all its surprising parallels woke her up.

The technical term we psychologists use for the transitional quality embedded within synchronistic events is *liminality*, which we have borrowed from anthropological studies on rites of passage. In traditional rites of passage, such as a child's initiation into adulthood by members of their tribe or various religious rituals that initiate or endow an individual with specific spiritual powers such as shamanistic healing or spiritual vision, Arnold Van Gennep, Mircea Eliade and other classic anthropologists described three phases. First, the initiate is brought out of their usual social context—abducted into the jungle, confined to a sacred hut or house—in essence, removed from the ordinary surroundings that represent the social status that they will be leaving behind in the course of their initiatory transformation. Second, they are kept in this place for sometimes an extended period of time in a betwixt-and-between state—no longer who they were but not yet initiated into who they will be—to which the term *liminal* was applied, drawn from the Latin word for threshold, *limen*. Both psychologically and socially, this middle, liminal phase of the process represents a time of maximum openness and creativity, happening as it often does in a place apart from the collective life of the tribe or social group, creating a place of freedom to experience in new ways previously unfelt spiritual energies, unconscious processes, new perspectives and/or a re-imagined relationship to others and to the natural world. Third and last, after this liminal phase has worked its effect on the initiate's sense of self—enlarging it, deepening it, definitively changing it—he or she is then brought back to the tribe, back into their original social context for re-integration.

One can see fairly easily why this description of the phases of traditional rites of passage drew the attention of those of us working in the more modern setting of psychotherapeutic change and transformation. Other than the fact that traditional rites of passage are usually involuntary and collective, whereas psychotherapy is (almost always) voluntary and individual in nature, the parallels are striking. First, those coming to therapy are highly motivated to be changed into someone else—leave an old self behind, whether due to illness, inauthenticity, or incompleteness—and become someone new, healed from illness or trauma, more fully realized and integrated in one's potential. Second, the psychotherapy office is very much a liminal place, a space apart, a social context privileged with a legally protected level of privacy and seclusion, in which the patient can freely open himself or herself to the exploration of what they might become. And finally, ideally, the end of the therapeutic endeavor is ultimately re-integration, the living out of that new, more authentic, healed sense of self, in love and in work, as Freud famously put it.

What tipped off us Jungians to the essential liminality of the therapeutic process was the extraordinary frequency of synchronistic events that occurred, not just throughout the course of our work with our clients but, for me particularly, the striking number of synchronistic events that occurred for me and the client *during* our actual psychotherapy sessions, some of which I recounted in *There Are No Accidents*. So when there was a power outage in the middle of my session with a client at the exact moment of his vociferously declaring his sense of powerlessness over his own life only to have all the lights go back on later in the session when he equally vociferously declared his intention to take back his power, or when a client of mine out of anger at my pushing him too hard in a session called me "a barker at the gates to Hell," only to have my dog in the next room start to bark incessantly outside our door and not stop for the rest of the session, I was helped immensely to appreciate the significance of such occurrences by Jung's classic story of synchronicity that had happened to him and his patient, oft told but still delightful and relevant as ever:

My example concerns a young woman patient who, in spite of efforts made on both sides, proved to be psychologically inaccessible. The difficulty lay in the fact that she always knew better about everything. Her excellent education had provided her with a weapon ideally suited to this purpose, namely a highly polished Cartesian rationalism with an impeccably "geometrical" idea of reality. After several fruitless attempts to sweeten her rationalism with a somewhat more human understanding, I had to confine myself to the hope that something unexpected and irrational would turn up, something that would burst the intellectual retort into which she had sealed herself. Well, I was sitting opposite her one day, with my back to the window, listening to her flow of rhetoric. She had an impressive dream the night before, in which someone had given her a golden scarab — a costly piece of jewelry. While she was still telling me this dream, I heard something behind me gently tapping on the window. I turned round and saw that it was a fairly large flying insect that was knocking against the window-pane from outside in the obvious effort to get into the dark room. This seemed to me very strange. I opened the window immediately and caught the insect in the air as it flew in. It was a scarabaeid beetle, or common rose-chafer (*Cetonia aurata*), whose gold-green colour most nearly resembles that of a golden scarab. I handed the beetle to my patient with the words, "Here is your scarab." This experience punctured the desired hole in her rationalism and broke the ice of her intellectual resistance. The treatment could now be continued with satisfactory results. (CW 8)

What Synchronicity Reveals About Our Families and The Self

One does not really, of course, need to explore the various stories of synchronistic events as thoroughly or in such detail as we have just done for such events to have the delightful or transformative effect that they generally have on us. That is, I think, part of their unusual quality, what makes these coincidences special occurrences in our lives. Without "making" them happen, the significance of these sorts of events—their emotional impact, symbolic quality and transitional effect—almost seems to just occur *to* us. That's why I think so many of us get annoyed or exasperated when telling the story of such amazing coincidences to people of a doubtful or unempathic bent who dismissively pronounce "you are just reading things into it" or "sure, that's crazy, but things like that happen all the time. You're making a lot out of it, aren't you?"

I'm happy to say here that I share your exasperation at such attitudes, and I daresay Jung would as well, because behind our experience of the seemingly spontaneous meaningfulness of a synchronistic event, Jung understood that one of the most important features of the human psyche was at work, our very capacity for psychological integration, our basic ability to make meaning at all through our ability to imagine and experience wholeness, completion, perfection. As he went about in his research and writings describing those universal aspects of human psychological experience he called "archetypes," Jung centered a great deal of his attention on the specific archetype which he ultimately called the "Self," that is, that universal capacity that lies in all of us to experience ourselves and our lives as whole and integrated.

Like all archetypes, which represent psychological capacities only occasionally and temporarily realized fully in our day-to-day experience, we go about our lives largely unconscious of the action of these psychological capacities as formed by our actual lived experiences. Though, of course, we have all had some experience of "mother" or "father" or "childhood" in some way—different in details from person to person, of course, but "mother," "father," "child" as a general pattern with distinct similarities overall across time and culture—as adults we do our business and engage in our relationships often largely unaware of how thoroughly those primal and universal human experience that we all share continue to affect us.

In Jung's words, we are, for the most part, *unconscious* of the *archetypal* level of this shared set of human experiences, so that level of experience therefore represents the *collective unconscious* of our human species. Jung was often criticized for the mysticism or vagueness of these, but as I think even my own short presentation above makes clear, all Jung was really doing was describing aspects of psychological experience we all universally share simply by virtue of our common humanity, and because we go about our lives not paying much attention to these universal and basic psychological experiences, they represent what is unconscious about ourselves, personally and collectively.

Some archetypes, like "mother" or "child," have an obvious personal quality but others represent more general aspects or situations: such is what Jung called the archetype of the Self. The capitalization of this term was, of course, not mere chance nor an artifact of German orthography. We each experience our little-s self in some way. We know who we are. We have a name. We experience the particularities of our bodies, our minds, our spirits. This is our conscious sense of "self," or what Jung called our "ego," the "I" that I am and experience as myself. But we also all have some sense of the relative limitedness of that little-s self, too, if we are honest with ourselves. We each *know* there is so much more to who we are that we can be aware of or fully feel at any given moment. There are ways we could be, things we could do, ideas we could think, accomplishments we could achieve—in short, a fully-integrated, realized, expanded wholeness of experience that we can all *imagine* manifesting ideally: not the self we are, but rather a Self, with a capital S, that we could be. And this supra-ordinate Self, as Jung put it, that capacity for wholeness—to see how all is connected in the universe around us and to see how we ourselves fit into that infinity of completion—is what is at work when we make meaning of the events of our lives.

Now, when we intentionally and assiduously turn our attention to deep reflection upon what it is that we have lived and what, therefore, it means—as we do in psychotherapy certainly but also in our religious or spiritual practices or as we do in the course of artistic expression— we are consciously and willingly activating the archetype of the Self within us. It is this active, larger Self which brings meaning out from behind the curtain of our inattention and unconsciousness and forward into the light of our self-awareness. The best of all human achievement, therefore, one might say, rests on the archetype of the Self, which is certainly why Jung himself spent nearly a third of his life and his writings exploring this particular archetype and its manifestations in the psychological life of individuals in the course of human history and religion.

Synchronistic events are yet another way we experience the Self— unintentionally, by surprise, without seeking or trying. When we are startled by the way in which we discover, by complete and unlikely chance, that our great-great-grandfather played the very same unusual musical instrument as we happen to be pursuing a career playing, we feel the connection immediately through the meaning-making capacity of the Self. The uncanny quality of such a synchronicity for our conscious mind lies precisely in the way that the significance of it isn't actually sought but, instead, *occurs to* our ego. It feels outside ourselves, because in a way it is: the Self is beyond the limitation of the ego, by definition, but it is not actually *outside* our psyche as a whole in some absolute way. Quite the contrary, while our conscious mind may experience the meaningful coincidence so spontaneously recognized at the moment as something *occurring to* us, it is crucial to understand that the significance of the event that we experience is actually due to the deeper archetypal wholeness, the Self with its meaning-making function, that lies *within* us.

All of the above is a long way of bringing us, at last, to the specific topic of this book, the stories of our families, or, to put it another way, why the synchronistic events within families herein each reveal a critical piece of something I believe is important to assert about the nature of families. In contrast to the common way I believe many of us think about what a family is—a collection of people related biologically through blood, over which such a literal and concrete understanding wars have been fought, feuds have been pursued, and all manner of human glory and shame has been made manifest—the synchronistic events within our family experience that have been told to me throughout the years emphasize the fundamentally psychological in nature of the "family" as a manifestation, maybe even arguably the most important, immediate, and universal manifestation, of the archetype of the Self, our psychological capacity to imagine and experience wholeness. We experience synchronicity in our family relationships *because* both synchronicity and our families manifest the Self as archetype of wholeness to us in ways that we do not "cause" but rather, instead, spontaneously experience as meaningful.

Of course, the "family" is on some level a biological reality and yes, of course, there is a level of conscious intentionality that is involved in the creation of our families. We do choose to enter into relationship, intend to have children, put effort into maintaining the ties we have with our families of origin and the extended family we belong to beyond our nuclear family. A client of mine from Texas used to call her own family—her kids and husband—her "little" family and referred to the wider family circle of her parents, grandparents, aunts, uncles and cousins as her "big" family, which is a description I've found myself adopting and using in the course of my practice as a marriage and family therapist.

"Big" or "small," however, the biological connections we might have with blood relatives do not in and of themselves, though, have any meaning or significance apart from the psychological, emotional or relational significance that we either give them—intentionally and consciously—or which we experience spontaneously and automatically—that is, unintentionally and unconsciously. But in either case, the psychological experience of family--conscious or unconscious—rests on the archetypal experience of wholeness which Jung called the Self. And it is specifically this unconscious, psychological foundation of our experience of family which all of the synchronistic experiences in the book make clear.

Our families are so critically important to who we are, because our family is the first place in our human experience that we first encounter the archetype of the Self in our lives. It is our first and most basic experience of belonging, connection, attachment, unity. That is why any early experience of deficiency or trauma within our families has such a deep and lasting impact on us for the rest of our lives. Were families really simply just a matter of biological connection, then inadequate parenting, neglect, abuse or any other forms of emotional or social deficiency or conflict experienced within our primary family would be simply repaired by merely distancing oneself physically from our families of origin.

However, the family is fundamentally, indeed, as I have said, an archetypal experience, and thus, the vicissitudes of our family history, small or big, resonate fundamentally within that area of our experience of self that constitutes our very ability to make sense and meaning of our lives as a whole. It is the archetypal level of our family experience that the stories of synchronicity here illustrate and bring forward, for those that lived them and for us who read them.

CHAPTER TWO

When Two Souls Meet: Synchronicity, Love and our Myths of Origin

All families—those we come from and those we create—are born out of relationship, and it is often these "myths of origin" which make up a large and cherished treasury of stories told from generation to generation. Ask anyone at a party "how did you meet your partner?" or "how did your parents meet?" and odds are that you will hear a tale, usually well-practiced in the telling, that clearly mixes together elements of delight and satisfaction. These stories are what root us in our history and remind us of the wonderful uniqueness of our individuality, for after all they "explain" how we came to be. For this reason, in many cultures these are sacred stories, and often the ritual telling goes back countless generations to the beginning of time. But in the end, whether it's a cocktail party "how we met" or the formal chanting of how our people descended from the gods, families grow from the encounter of two people in love.

And the encounter of two people who fall in love and enter into relationship, particularly a relationship like marriage out of which the new lives of children are born and raised, very naturally always has about it a sense of the magical and mystical. As Jung famously said about the analytic relationship, but it is certainly true about all relationships, "the meeting of two personalities is like the contact of two chemical substances: if there is any reaction, both are transformed." It is precisely this transformative quality of relationship which lends to our stories of meeting the sense of wonder and infuses both our reflections on the circumstances and our telling of the event with a common human joy. We are born of relationship, as humans, and it is our relatedness which brings us to an awareness of what we share with everyone on the planet.

However, it must be said that not every meeting between two people, not every love relationship or marriage, is entirely random nor especially, dramatically, coincidental or synchronistic. In the course of my now long professional career and during my even longer time on the earth, I would say that the vast majority of relationships I've had or have counseled grew out of entirely logical connections and common-alities between two people. My friends Tony and Rose grew up near one another, were a couple in high school, got married soon after and just a few months ago at my 40th high school reunion, they were there together still, having raised their family and looking altogether content with one another. Likewise, a couple recently came to see me for a relationship tune-up around their communications. They had met through church circles, felt attracted to one another, discovered things in common, had a similar vision of what they wanted their lives to look like, and so eventually got married, raised a family, and now, as empty nesters, came to me for a spot of help in the process of rediscovering each other 25 years later now that the kids were launched into their own happy and productive lives.

Indeed, most of our relationships and families have, I would say, this sort of entirely normal and natural developmental trajectory, in which the elements of chance do play some part, the circumstances of our birth, the individual elements of what we feel drawn toward and why. And of course, there are even less chance-laden stories of relationship than these, for after all, we all know folks in our lives who actually set about quite intentionally to find a relationship, to get married, who had quite clear and fixed ideas of what it is they wanted in a husband or wife, and set about taking advantage of all the latest social-network technology at our fingertips to snag their soulmate. If you put up a profile on a dating site with clear criteria as to what you're attracted to in a partner, and then assiduously go about dating only such people as meet those criteria, we might say that the element of chance plays some part when you meet Mr. or Ms. Right—they happened to see your profile, they happened to respond—but ultimately, there was an intentionality about the process that makes the meeting a good deal less than random.

When I tell the story about how I met my own partner Paul, both the incremental/developmental aspect and the somewhat intentional aspect play a part. I was coming to California for grad school at age 22, had broken up with my boyfriend, was eager to date, had come across a flyer for a seminarians conference in Berkeley the very month I would be arriving, touched down, called the Graduate Theological Union who put me in touch with the man who was organizing it, said, "sure, let's meet," when he suggested I come to his office on Virginia Street, introduced himself as Paul, noticed the mutual attraction, and went out on a date during which we discovered a ton of mutual things in common, both on the level of life experiences and values. From there, the rest was history.

But none of it, I would say, was especially synchronistic, and that was largely because there was so much of our own consciousness and agency that had been brought to bear in the process. I was actively open to meeting someone, indeed, sought out the connection, and of course was certainly delighted by the things we ended up sharing, not just in the meeting but for the thirty-three years we spent together before his death, but the element of chance did not play much a role.

On the other hand, in the several decades since the publication of my first book, people have told me stories of meeting their partners wherein an entirely other quality of encounter comes into play. Here the relationship *happens to* a person—which itself is a curious notion, I think—and this most important of all relationships, out of which their own family and generations of eventual descendants emerge, this primary relationship is actually from its origin unsought, unplanned and even at times, unwanted. Now, these are the stories which, as a student of the unconscious soul, I find especially intriguing, not just for the dramatics of them but because of what they disclose about our complexity. For these synchronistic stories of meetings demonstrate that some of us connect even if we are not looking to connect, even if we make no provision, space or time in our lives to engage with another lovingly, intimately, intensively. In fact, even if we are at a certain point actively resisting relationship—traumatized from childhood, wounded from a recent breakup, or characterologically avoidant of involvements—or in a less emotionally charged fashion, just simply uninterested in being distracted by the energy another person requires, motivated far more by other gratifications such as our career, our interests, our creative process, *still* we may find ourselves brought together by sheer synchronistic chance with the person with whom we will be spending our lives.

In the course of many of the stories I have been told over the years, I've found the synchronistic meetings between two people who ended up being spouses, life partners and parents of a family fall into roughly two categories: synchronicities of circumstance and synchronicities of commonality. In the first, the circumstances of the meeting are what seemed to be shot through with elements of chance, wherein someone found themselves, I might say, "in the wrong place at the right time" which becomes a retrospective source of wonder. "What if...." is the question these tales bring forward. In the second, the synchronistic quality of the encounter is revealed not through the original circumstance but an entirely coincidental set of commonalities—shared histories, dates, times, places and experiences—that over time gradually get woven into a sense that the relationship almost was "meant to be." These are the slow-moving synchronicities in which a series of events slowly builds into a coherence, into a story we originally didn't even know we were inhabiting.

The Right Place at the Right Time: Synchronicities of Circumstance

The story of how Massimo Bottura, celebrated Italian chef of Osteria Francescana in Modena, met and eventually married his wife Lara is a classic story of romantic synchronicity and stands as an excellent example of how chance, sometimes welcome, sometimes unwelcome, becomes a factor in shaping our life story. As they tell it in the episode of *Chef's Table*, Massimo had already begun his career in Modena with a small restaurant and had met with middling success. A creative type, he has a sense of restlessness about him as he recounts his successes in his first restaurant.

"After a couple of years, Campazzo was successful so I said to my partner, I'm going to leave and spend some time living in New York, away from Campazzo, and I left. One day I was walking in Soho and I wanted to get a great coffee, so I saw this restaurant, I walk in to get an espresso, but I had to wait 20 minutes. So, I said to myself, hmmm, maybe they have some problems here. I said to them, if you need some help, I can help you. I went back home and found the owner had left a message for me. 'Massimo, if you please, can you come tomorrow for the shift from two until closing time, that will be great.'"

Lara's side of the story is not entirely different, as she, too, wanders into the same restaurant with not that different an experience. "I was in New York living in the East Village, and one day I stop into this little cafe called Caffè di Nonna. I had an interview with the owner and told him that I spoke Italian and knew how to make a cappuccino. By the time I got back to my apartment in the East Village, I had a message on my answering machine that said, 'Could you please tomorrow and do a trial shift?'"

The end result was a chance encounter that would eventually end up changing their entire lives, for both Massimo and Lara literally walk into one another reporting to work for their first time, on the same schedule, two until closing. Their attraction to one another is immediate and, as they tell the story, the intimate space they are sharing in this small one-room restaurant only enhances their feelings—Lara staffing the bar across the room from the open-kitchen set-up where Massimo is behind the counter, making some of the best Italian food she had ever eaten, food, as she puts it, that was so "simple, so direct, it went right to the heart. It won me over." Meanwhile, the irrepressible Massimo, clearly enjoying his break from the responsibilities of restaurant owner, goes about his work with characteristic humor and style, and slowly the two of them fall in love.

However, what might have been easy, boy, girl, love, marriage, ends up becoming suddenly, by sheer happenstance, much, much more complicated. "Then, out of the blue," Massimo says, raising his eyes to the heavens and asking the question, "out of the blue? I received a phone that I need to go back to reality…I had to go back to Modena."

The separation takes its toll, for, as we can well imagine, absence only made their hearts grow fonder, and without all the conveniences of modern internet social networking, the way they ended up staying in touch was through the occasional (and expensive) phone call but usually through the much cheaper fax machine of yore, with Lara sending him little drawings and updates about what was happening across the Atlantic in New York, and Massimo now and then grabbing the time to fax or call back, until one day, she gets a fax that asks, quite simply: "When are you coming to Modena?"

Desperately in love with the man and without any clear idea about the long-term plans of how to make any of it work, Lara nevertheless packs up and moves her life to Modena, only once again to have their life together turned upside down by yet another random event in Massimo's professional life.

"After about a week from when I arrived in Modena, Massimo then gets this crazy call from Alain Ducasse. It was the end of 1993, everyone is talking about this big famous chef, and Alain said to Massimo, 'Would you like to come to Hotel de Paris, it would be honor to have you there, to teach our staff how to prepare homemade pasta, how to make tortellini.'" It was an incredible opportunity and Massimo was over the moon. Me, on the other hand, I had just arrived, only ten days had gone by, and all of a sudden Massimo's world is being turned upside down and he's leaving!"

The expression on her face makes clear the difficulties this presented to them. "We had one of those long horrible conversations, and I wanted to know should I stay or should I go. To which he says, 'You know, Lara, I dated a girl for so many years before I met you, and how can I make a choice like this now?" And I thought, 'Oh, that's great. That sucks.' So, he sold Campazzo and he left, after which I said to myself, 'You know, you have to get on with your life,' so I just got a flight back to New York."

Having listened for three decades to couples tell the story of how they met, fell in love and decided, eventually, to marry and start their families, I know the silence that then ensues between them in their interview speaks volumes. But then, out of the blue—out of the blue?—Massimo continues by telling the story of another, apparently unrelated culinary accident. "So, there I was, in Monaco, and Taka my sous chef is about to serve the last two lemon tarts, and suddenly, he drops one of the two tarts, and we were ready to serve them. And the tart had fallen on the counter, half on the plate, half on the counter. Taka was just white, he wanted to kill himself, commit hari kari. But I said, "Taka, stop. Stop! Look at it. That is beautiful. Let's rebuild it as if it were supposed to be broken up. Immediately, though he didn't understand, he trusted me so much and he said, "ok" so we get the lemon zabaglione and we just splash it on the plate like this," he gestures wildly, "but then we get the other elements and we rebuild them on top with precision to make it feel like we did it all on purpose. And that was the moment in which we created Oops, I Dropped the Lemon Tart!

"That day, I learned something. That in life, to move forward, you need to learn from your mistakes. Maybe I did something wrong, but you learn from it. So that was when, there in Monte Carlo, I realized the mistakes I had made with Lara, and I knew then I had to go, I had to be there with her. So, I said to Chef Ducasse, "I have things I have to take care, I have personal business. And it's been a great experience, but I need to go."

At which point, once again, with his unusual combination of creative restlessness and decisive clarity, he takes a flight directly to New York, goes to Lara to declare once and for all that he wants to be with her, for good, and that really he is willing to do whatever she wishes, just as long as they can be together, which is how the two of them ended up moving back to Modena and eventually working together to create Osteria Francescana, the sometimes shocking, always whimsical and idiosyncratic restaurant that introduced to a very tradition-bound Italian culinary scene a new way of approaching the experience of sharing a meal.

Certain aspects of Lara and Massimo's love story appear again and again in synchronistic stories of "how we met." First, it is striking that, wholly independently of one another, each of them end up crossing the threshold of the same place at the same time for the first time and literally bumping into one another on the doorstep. I would venture to say that all of us in our relationship have eventually come to realize the uniqueness of our partner, the one-in-a-million chance it has been that we should have come to know this person who so completely suits us, with whom we share so many things in common, who has that special kind of affinity or understanding for pieces of who we are, such that we decide, with time, "yes, he is the one," or "she's the only one for me." However, what a synchronistic story of meeting seems to have is that extra factor of a uniqueness of circumstance. Looking back, the timing was perfect and could not have been planned.

And yet, much like fairy tales and novels, we hear from these two real people that circumstance does not always cooperate with our own best-laid mortal plans, and quickly, in major ways, chance seems to be the enemy. Just when things are going so well, Massimo needs to leave, and not just once—called back to Modena—but even more infelicitously and wrenchingly, a second time, just days after Lara lands in Modena to join him. Here, too, however, the "bad" timing of this seems, interestingly enough, just as synchronistic to me, that is to say, ultimately full of a great deal of meaning and impact, not, obviously because it jived with our lovers' plans and expectations but rather precisely because it did not. Here, the random circumstance of an offer he couldn't refuse which took him away once more introduced an unwelcome but extraordinarily important element to their consciousness: the distance sharpened their awareness, and in particular, Massimo's awareness, of how much Lara meant to him and how what he had done had been, in fact, a mistake.

Naturally, the symbol Chef Bottura uses in his story to signal this shift in consciousness is drawn from the world of food, and what is clear to even the least perspicacious listener in his tale that when he tells the story of the creation of his signature dessert, Oops, I Dropped the Lemon Tart, he is not talking just about pastry. He is talking about the delicate, delicious, sweet container of the relationship so painstakingly created and then impulsively, even somewhat thoughtlessly, dropped and broken. A chance event, an accident, and yet, like all of the other "accidents" in this story, not an accident and here is the lesson: for what transformed the dropped and ruined tart from a mess fit for the garbage into a wholly wonderful delight that becomes the hallmark of his culinary life is his ability to see the accident in a new light, to draw from the chaos a beauty, and with conscious intention to rebuild something new that acknowledges both the accident and the commitment to a new vision, a lovely synthesis of random and intentional. Thus, he goes to New York, he and Lara decide after all the vicissitudes of their first year together to bring it all together, and from that union grows the family they create with one another, both inside and outside the restaurant they have now run together as husband and wife for 25 years.

It is an evocative image that we are offered in this story, the profundity of which might be hidden with Massimo's playful title— oops, I broke it! And the aptness of his image goes right to the heart of how most of us experience the action of chance in our lives—not as the delightful plot twist or the welcome opportunity for personal growth but rather, I would dare to say, as a very unwelcome intrusion into our plans and projects, the very thing we do *not* want to happen. Chance is what we seek to eliminate with our schedules and assiduity. Chance is what dis-integrates, breaks and smashes.

And yet, it is the artist in Chef Bottura, the possibilities that brokenness creates, which sees what the Japanese art of *kintsugi* or *kintsukuroi* has raised to an entire aesthetic. Literally meaning "golden joinery" or "golden repair," this particular form of art takes a broken piece of pottery and repairs it along the broken seams in such a way as to heighten the break, usually with golden lacquer that has been mixed with gold, silver or platinum, so that in the finished, repaired and restored piece of ceramic, the cracks actually stand out. Behind the utility of this sort of artwork and its unexpected beauty, which would be enough visually for certain, there is an even deeper meaning, a philosophy that animates this practice. As Christine Bartlett puts it, "Not only is there no attempt to hide the damage, but the repair is literally illuminated... a kind of physical expression of the spirit of *mushin*.... Mushin is often literally translated as 'no mind,' but carries connotations of fully existing within the moment, of non-attachment, of equanimity amid changing conditions.... The vicissitudes of existence over time, to which all humans are susceptible, could not be clearer than in the breaks, the knocks, and the shattering to which ceramic ware too is subject. This poignancy or aesthetic of existence has been known in Japan as *mono no aware*, a compassionate sensitivity, or perhaps identification with, [things] outside oneself" (*Flickwerk: The Aesthetics of Mended Japanese Ceramics*).

As applied to our relationships, therefore, Chef Bottura's insight and the wisdom of *kintsugi* makes clear that when chance intervenes, we are then faced with a choice: do we let the separation stand? Do we allow the operation of random events to sweep us away from those we love? Or do we use our will, our creativity, our consciousness to bring a new and different wholeness to the situation, acknowledging what has been and yet rebuilding, repairing, re-integrating in a way that respects both the brokenness of the past and the newness of the future?

One of the more delightful qualities of these romantic synchronicities is that they really throw a light into the particular wonder it actually is to find someone with whom we "click." In the everyday world of our family relationships in which we get up each day and find ourselves moving forward to simply take care of the day's business—making breakfast, getting the kids to school, and ourselves to work; presentable, on time, and focused; battling commuter traffic home, figuring out how to balance the necessities of family life with personal time and relaxation—it's not hard to lose touch with the special, even extraordinary, series of chances and circumstances that went into our finding a partner or spouse. These stories remind us, I think, that even if our own meeting wasn't a high-order-of-magnitude coincidence, it is still a rather amazing thing, and an occasion of gratitude, to find love and to have that love become the basis for a family of our own. That is the psychological and emotional meaning, I would say, of such stories of origin—to remind us of the wonder of the beginnings to illuminate and refresh our appreciation of what might otherwise seem a humdrum present.

When I put out a call for stories among my friends and colleagues, that delight is what came through most prominently with fellow therapist Joanna when we crossed paths at the agency where I volunteer. "You know, I got your email about the synchronicity stories and I wanted to talk to you. I don't know how dramatic this is but you know, the story of how my grandparents met was one of those things that is told over and over in my family, and I would say it was synchronistic before they even was a thing called synchronicity. I mean literally!"

I laughed, "Literally?"

She nodded. "Given that it occurred during World War II, yes, literally. Jung didn't even invent the word until 1950, right?"

That I had to give to her. "Correct. So how did they meet?"

She grabbed me and we went out onto the back deck. "Well, so, there are kind of two parts to it—there's the actual story and there's what I would call the 'mythic function' of the story in our family. It was a little bit like a fairy tale for us kids when my grandmother would tell it, and it's one of those stories I can't even remember when I heard the first time.

"So, the story goes that my grandfather was in the Navy during World War II. Young guy, nice-looking, lots of pictures of him in the albums with him in his blues, stationed here, in fact in Alameda, and basically fighting in the Pacific. So, between deployments, he ends up with a week in San Francisco on leave with his Navy buddies. Now he's doing what you would expect a guy his age to be doing on leave in San Francisco, and as he told it, he was pretty footloose and fancy free in those days. No commitments, not really looking for a girlfriend. He'd tell us that his experience in the Navy was great but that we kids couldn't really understand the level of uncertainty the entire world war had thrown everyone into. The United States had been bombed, no one really knew the outcome, it just wasn't a time for settling down, not to mention he himself was enjoying the freedom of being in the service, and particularly the Navy, seeing places he never would have seen otherwise, even if it was overall a dicey situation in terms of his safety. He grew up in the San Joaquin Valley, so being on the water, being away from my great-grandparents, fighting for his country, all of it was working for him as a young man.

"Shore leave in San Francisco with his buddies was pretty much what you would expect: lots of going out on the town. So, the group of them—him and his two other buddies—decide for their last night on leave they are going to this sailors' bar over somewhere in North Beach, and for whatever reason, they are all going to meet there separately. My grandfather ends up going to this place, it's a Friday night, everyone's out having a great time, and he waits and he waits. No friends. Now that doesn't stop him from having a few, of course, and as the night goes on, he's having a fine time but still his friends don't show up, which is pretty weird because these three are tight with one another. They are on the same ship, they have each other's backs in combat. As my grandfather would say, they're not showing up was pretty out of character and, periodically throughout the evening, he's thinking that something might be wrong, maybe he should leave, go back to the rooming house where they were staying, you know, look for them, and a couple of times he almost does that but by then, he's enjoying himself, he's made some friends, he's telling Navy stories, he's impressing the girls.

"Anyway, the night gets late, and he's about to head out when he literally stumbles over the doorstep on his way out just as these two young ladies are coming in, and the woman who ends up being my grandmother actually literally catches him. Now, of course, when they used to tell the story to us kids, they made it into a bit of a fairy tale, love at first sight. My grandfather actually used to say, 'I looked up and there she was, my angel who caught me.' As I've gotten older, naturally, I realize that this was a little bit of poetic license on their parts, which really is sort of cute, but the fact was he *was* leaving and he actually tripped and fell right into her. So that's how they met. She thought he was handsome, so when he offered to buy her and her sister a drink that evening and make the night last a little bit longer, she didn't refuse, and in the end, they ended up really hitting it off.

"It's his last night of leave, though, so they swap addresses, neither of them really knowing when or how they will ever see each other again, and off he goes. He gets back to where they were staying and as it turns out, the reason that his friends weren't there was because my grandfather had actually gone to the *wrong* bar that night. They had all agreed to go to this place they had gone earlier that week, but for some reason, my grandfather got it into his head that they had agreed to go to the place in North Beach where he went, but really, they hadn't. So, he really shouldn't have been there, but of course, because he was, he met my grandmother, who ended up writing him for the rest of his time in the service, and eventually at the end of the war, he decided to set himself here in the Bay Area to be with her."

Joanne paused a bit and smiled. "We kids always loved this story, of course, it's pretty romantic but my grandfather and grandmother also used it as a little bit of family folk wisdom whenever we'd get upset about things not going our way or when we would be hard on ourselves about screwing things up or when people didn't come through for us. It was one of those things he'd sometimes say." And here she imitated her grandfather's voice. "'Well, you know, sweetheart, if I hadn't screwed up where I was supposed to meet my friends, I never would have met your grandmother, and you wouldn't be here.' or 'You know, if my friends had been there the night I met your grandmother, who knows, I may never have met her.'

"So that's what I mean when I say the story had a kind of purpose to it. It was a bit of a teaching lesson for us kids about being open to how what's happening now may not be what we think it is. And I do love how he'd always end his little lecture by saying, 'and you know, if I had been in the right place, you wouldn't be here!'"

Joanna's charming story about how her grandparents met reassures us that before Jung even came up with the word "synchronicity," synchronistic events were bring people together. Hank's story, on the other hand, provides a bit of a proof that in a globalized era of the Internet in which our love lives are now permeated by online social networking, the archetypes of the collective unconscious are alive and well and still expressing themselves through the plethora of all the electronic media at our fingertips.

"It's weird how I met my boyfriend," Hank said to me on the phone when I spoke with him. "Maybe the kind of thing that only happens these days, and I do sometimes think, how would I have ever met Jim if we didn't have all these gadgets. But still it's a little strange how it happened.

"I don't know, it's about five or six years ago, and this friend of mine at work tells me about this online app he got on his phone called Grindr, which they are calling a dating app, wink wink, but in fact is really a kind of hookup app. At the time I remember thinking, 'really, what will they come up with next?' because I mean they are all these online dating sites and I even had a Match.com profile at the time and met a few guys through there, but here's this Grindr thing now and you can actually see who is within literally 100 feet of you. It really did blow my mind a little bit, but then I start talking to friends and it turns out everyone's using it. So naturally, me, too, I download the thing to my phone, set up my profile with a nice pic of myself, and I start browsing, and you know, it's like five minutes and of course I get all kinds of messages from some pretty hot guys, but I've never really been into the whole anonymous sex thing and it turns out, of course, that it's not *really* a dating app. These guys aren't looking for Mr. Right, they aren't even pretending to look for Mr. Right, they are looking for Mr. Right Now, and pretty much interested in Mr. Who's Around the Corner, 728 Feet Away From Me, Right Now. Anyway, it was a bit of a hoot, especially when I'd go into the city out of the suburbs, I mean suddenly there are dozens and dozens of gay guys geolocated, and really nice-looking guys, don't get me wrong, but like I said, hooking up with strangers on the fly just wasn't my style.

"So then, I realize that there's a place where you can adjust your location on this app, so that instead of showing you who's where you are at the moment, you can input your zip code and the app will show you who's near you in that location, so that, let's say you are going to be traveling to Boston tomorrow, you input a Boston zip code, and then suddenly all the guys within the vicinity of that zip code pop-up. Handy little tool to make advance plans so you aren't at a loose end in a strange town," Hank said with a bit of a wry tone.

"So, really, out of sheer curiosity, I in fact input the zip code of my old apartment in Washington DC, just to see who pops up there, and there are quite a number of nice looking gentleman, and one in particular, Jim, messages me, and unlike most of them on there, he doesn't come across as sleazy or pushy or oversexual, just seems to want to chat, so we have a decent enough conversation and at that point I tell him that I'm actually not in DC but up in New Jersey, but that I went to school in DC, etc. etc. So that's that, and you know, at that point I really didn't think twice about it or him, and in fact, after a while, I got sort of tired of the dumb thing sending me all of these notifications which are all just guys who want to hook up so I delete the app from my phone altogether and live a much quieter online life for a while.

"Anyway, maybe, I don't know, six months later, they come up with a new one of these things, again, marketed as a dating app, this one is called Scruff, so Mr. Curiosity, I download that one, set it up, and after a while, it's more or less the same kind of thing. This one is a little less hook-uppy and the guys' profiles aren't so upfront-sexual, it does seem like a little bit more date-oriented, but as I scroll down, you know, checking out the guys located farther and farther away from me, I get to Philadelphia and who do I see there but Jim, the guy from DC that I had chatted with earlier that year on Grindr--same pic, same profile--only now he's on Scruff. I remember he was a nice guy and maybe we chatted few times back then, so I message him and say hi. As it happens, he actually remembers me, and I ask him what he's doing in Phila-delphia, and he has actually moved there for work. He's a teacher, the job he had in DC was a contract position, it ended in June, and he found himself a job in Philly teaching starting that fall. So, now he's close enough where actually meeting him isn't ridiculous, but I'm not really thinking that way. I'm just doing this Scruff thing as a little bit of online fun, and he's not pushing it either from his end, so we end up having a nice online chat for a couple of weeks, I would say, checking up on each other in the morning, nothing really sexual, though I will say I found *that* particularly attractive. He seemed like just a normal person, not a big sleazeball, teacher, has a dog, goes to work, so on and so forth.

"Anyway, same deal with Scruff eventually on my side. I keep getting these obnoxious messages from guys who are only interested in sex, a lot of times obviously on drugs, and though I did connect online with a few really nice-seeming guys through it, and even went on a couple of dates with guys I met, the online thing sort of lost its charm, and I end up deleting this one, too.

"But of course, online life knows no end of development, and now I see through my regular old Facebook this thing called Instagram. People are posting pictures of themselves, and of course, what they are having for lunch and dinner, pics of their cats, flowers, workout photos, you name it, through this Instagram thing. So, like everyone else, I download this one, and you know, I post my pics, some of them normal, some of them a little, I guess you would say, provocative, you know, I'm wearing a Speedo, or like my leather outfit for Halloween, normal gay guy stuff, no nudity. And here, people 'follow' you, so who pops up among my followers but this guy Jim, again with the same picture he had on Grindr and then on Scruff. Only this time he messages me. And he's like, "Guess what?" So, I'm all, "What?" And he tells me he's not in Philadelphia anymore but in fact is living in the same town as me, and not just that, but, the truly bizarre thing is, he is teaching in the elementary school that is literally around the corner from my house.

"So that was a little mind-blowing, and that night, after having chatted with him for a couple of years across two different apps on the phone, we ended up meeting for dinner, really hitting it off and we've been together ever since. I just thought the whole thing was so strange, really, and in a way, maybe not so much. After all, with these apps, it's like we can connect to people everywhere all around the world with a tap, so in some ways, the possibility of connecting with someone like Jim is not just possible but maybe more likely than ever. I'm sure there are a bazillion people who've met their partners through online these days, but really what are the chances that he'd end up actually working around the corner from me and we'd end up crossing paths on yet another completely different online app? Were we meant to be together? I'd have to say yes to that, given our story."

It is, of course, the peculiarly perfect timing of all of these meetings which makes these stories both delightful and somewhat novelistic. Though screenwriters and fiction writers enjoy using the trope of a chance meeting, the urgency of temporal circumstance and the fragile window of timing to create tension and lay the foundation for a subsequent dramatic, happy ending for their couples in love, what such real stories as the Botturas', Joanna's or Hank's makes clear is that, as much as art imitate life, life often returns the favor and imitates art when we meet our soul mates.

Given the theme of this book, though, which is centered upon the nature of coincidence, I'm also struck by how these stories of coincidence in turn disclose the nature of time itself. When and if we think about time at all, we tend to think in our modern age about time as an objective reality or even consider it one of the fundamental physical properties of reality itself, what with Einstein's theory of relativity and his pioneering insights into the intimate interrelationship of energy, matter, space and time as separate dimensions of but one, singular reality. And yet, however objective and physical the nature of time may be for the physicist, our stories, and especially these sorts of family stories, show me the psychotherapist that our experience of time is for all its objective and even quasi-material reality just as much a subjective and immaterial reality as well. They may seem on their face simple family stories of "how I met my partner" but these stories actually only *become* important in the course of time, in the light of subsequent historical events: "how I met my partner" is "how our family got started" which is *why* the random chance of the encounter at the beginning takes on the meaning that it has. We might say that it acquires that meaning retrospectively, but it's slightly more accurate to say that it is the course of time that eventually rendered the initial encounter meaningful for those involved. It is the subsequent history that grew out of this encounter, the family that this meeting created with the passage of time, that then made the coming-together of these two people so felicitous and momentous.

Students of mythology and comparative religions know that all cultures have their myths of origin. The book of Genesis, the Kumulipo of the native Hawaiians, the Cosmogony of Hesiod--these are some of the great myths of creation, and they are told over and over by generation after generation, transmitted down through history, as a way of connecting the present moment, we who are now, with the infinity of human experience, who we will always be. So, too, are these smaller and more personal "myths of origin" about how I met my spouse, and the synchronistic nature of some of these meetings arises directly out of the transcendental experience of encountering a reality greater than ourselves in the experience of love. Here, we *know* the Self is at work, because the timing of the meeting feels so right, and thus, this palpable link between ourselves and the eternity of love becomes elaborated in a cherished family story that explains how it all began.

Or to say it another way, our experience of the infinite is not out there nor outside of history, but right there within our own experience of family. These stories of meaningful coincidence that brought two people together in love show how this experience of time is within us and ensconced in history, indeed it *becomes* our family's history from which important psychological lessons, the wisdom of life, can be drawn. The Botturas came together in love as a couple despite obstacles and, as they tell their family's myth of origin, the meaning of their synchronistic encounter is clear: what is broken can be made beautiful, if you bring your full self to it with intention and creativity. Joanna's family story likewise was, as she said, literally and deliberately used as a teaching example by her parents and grandparents: make no presumptions about the outcome when things appear not to be going your way, there may be hidden and transformative blessings in your 'bad luck.' Hank's story of growing closer—literally as well as emotionally—to the man that would become his eventual partner in life came to encapsulate a lesson for him about openness, wonder and persistence.

Such stories show us, as I said from the start, the intersection of the archetypal nature of family and the foundation of the synchronistic experience in the experience of wholeness and completion, which is why in my opinion, they take on the character of a "family legend." Thereby, they become sources of wisdom and grounding, serving for the smaller culture of our families a function not at all unlike the function of grounding and guiding that the grander myths of origin serve for the larger cultures and broader groups of peoples or nations.

Put another way yet again, what I perceive in these stories of synchronistic meetings, these family myths of origin, is that characteristic of time which is disclosed by our experience of archetypal reality and, in the final analysis, only possible to have subjectively: namely, how the present moment is infinity, simultaneously now and forever. After all, these meetings did occurred literally and at quite specific times and places—indeed, the specificity of those circumstances comes through loud and clear as the very stuff of the narrative, the year, the place, what we ate, what was said—but it's the synchronistic quality of the coming together and what it meant, that makes those concrete and literal specifics in time and space the endless reality of the relationship between these two individuals in love, to be told and retold across the decades at the start of "our family."

The One: Synchronicities of Commonality

That said, as we have all experienced in our lives, I daresay, the course of true love never runs smoothly. While the synchronistic circumstances of some couples' meetings had the result of starting off their relationship under the light of what seems to be a constellation of benign stars all quite unexpectedly lining up to bring these two lovers together now and forever, the more ordinary circumstance is that we meet and get to know each other more slowly and gradually, a process is generally much more fraught with legitimate questions. Is he the one? Can I completely trust her? I'm attracted on one level but do we really share enough? Most times this natural uncertainty in the beginning stages of relationship eventually resolves itself over time and with greater intimacy born, ideally, of honest conversation, deeper acquaintance, and a patiently constructed life together of shared experiences.

But after many years of exploring synchronistic events with my clients, readers, friends and family, there are times where in addition to the organic growth of emotional intimacy between two people, certain surprising and significant synchronistic events have brought home to a couple the way in which yes, indeed, they seemed to be "meant for one another." These synchronicities of commonality, as I have come to call them, often function to spark an awareness in a person of what they may indeed share with this intriguing stranger, this friend of a friend, this co-worker they keep crossing paths with, who may—and then does—become their life partner.

For example, a reader from England wrote whom I'll call Evelyn wrote me a brief but lovely story of how she had met her husband on a train on her way to London from Cambridge, where she, an expatriate American had moved to the UK for academic studies in medieval English poetry. "At the time, I would say what I was doing was quite obscure, and not at all in the mainstream, so I was taken aback when I saw this rather good-looking young Chinese man in the same compartment as I, reading a collection of the very sort of poetry which was the field of my study. That gave me an opportunity to strike up a conversation. When I asked him what his interest was in these rather dusty old bards, he told me he thought it might help him learn English better if he took a comprehensive, historical approach to how the language developed. Had it not been for his reading that book which was the very focus of my study, I doubt he and I would have ever crossed paths, the two of us are from such different worlds."

Sometimes the synchronicity of commonalities, though, don't begin at the start of the relationship but are only revealed over time and have more to do with the past than the present. One of the interns at the agency where I serve as clinical supervisor, Jeremy, wrote to me about a network of shared experiences and near misses that he and his partner of the past four years found out about only after they had been begun their relationship.

Jeremy writes, "I was born in 1980 in Wilmington, North Carolina, but my family had only just moved there from Utica, NY, when my father accepted a faculty position in the psychology department at University of North Carolina. And like most academic families, we then moved from there, Wilmington, to Baltimore, Maryland, eight years later in 1988, when my father accepted a staff position in the psychology department at Johns Hopkins University.

"So fast-forward, many years later. When my partner and I met in May of 2012, inevitably we talked about our life histories and the topic of where we came and where we had lived, at which point he told me that he had just moved to San Francisco in 2011, after a full 23 years of living in Wilmington and that in fact, he had moved there in 1988 to pursue and obtain a degree in psychology. In other words, we realized that he moved to Wilmington the same year we left and had moved there to pursue a degree in psychology, specifically, my father's department at UNCW, so he only narrowly missed having my father as his advisor! Plus, as we talked further, it turned out that, equally coincidentally, while we were living in Wilmington, my mother was teaching at Cape Fear Tech (now Cape Fear Community College), and this is the school where my partner eventually obtained his nursing degree to become a registered nurse.

"So naturally, with all these past interconnections, on a visit to my sister's house early in our relationship, the two of them were talking about possible mutual friends they might have had, since they are about the same age, at which point, they realize that they both went to the same science/math sleepover camp in North Carolina when they were both in 8th grade or so, and though they don't recall meeting each other they did in fact have some mutual friends from summer camp."

If Jeremy and his partner were still living in Wilmington and pursuing similar professional goals as psychotherapist and nurse, respectively, both of which grew out of family backgrounds in those fields, I don't know if we might be entirely surprised at such coincidences. We might chalk it all up to "small college town" and your basic "networking." However, that Jeremy's partner—whom he met clear across the country here in California—had nearly crossed paths with his whole family many years before the two of them even knew one another makes their subsequent discovery the kind of confirmatory synchronicity that ends up becoming part of a family's repository of stories.

Another "what we share" account, bringing home in a synchronistically romantic way the rightness of being together, comes from my friend Nessie. "Long before I met Ramon, I worked as an EMT in Sacramento, which is where I grew up. Very intense work. That's why I don't do it any longer. Anyway, I come down here, get my degree, pursue my career in marketing the way I'm doing now, and through friends, Ramon and I meet and we start dating. Turns out we're both from Sacramento. Turns out that his parents still live there. So that's not too coincidental, and of course I eventually tell him that I did EMT work up there, and so on and so forth.

"Anyway, we start getting serious, and it's time to go meet the folks, which is good because everyone is in Sacramento, very convenient. I introduce him to mine first one weekend, and it goes well, but then, the next weekend, we start heading over to his parents' place and I realize, oh my God, I've actually been here. So, as we are pulling up, I say to him, 'Did your father have a heart attack, I don't know, maybe ten years ago?' and he's like, 'Yeah, he did.'

"So, as it turns out I was on the call for his father's heart attack, which I tell him, but I'm thinking maybe he thinks I'm making it up, so I say, 'let's not say anything.' So, when we go in and he introduces me to his mom, she's over there, like looking at me, and I play with her a little and I say, 'Do we know one another?' And she's thinking and thinking, 'You look really familiar.' Well, finally I tell her, 'Remember when your husband had that heart attack, I was on the emergency team that came here. In fact, I rode to the hospital with you in the ambulance.'

"It was pretty incredible. His dad was out of it, of course, that night, he didn't remember me at all, he didn't know what was happening, but his mom definitely realized that it was me. So weird, really. But Ramon and I thought it was a sign, you know. And his dad even says, 'Nessie saved my life,' which I didn't really, but it is very sweet to think that I was part of the family in a way before I was really even part of the family."

Whereas Jeremy and Nessie tell of certain aspects of their mutual history they shared without knowing it, another place in our lives where a stroke of meaningful coincidence can sometimes occur in a way that cements the depth of connection early in relationship is around actual material objects or gifts. I myself became interested in this particular sort of occurrence between couples, in which a gift is given or received in a synchronistic way, when I realized that I had had a number of such coincidences occur to me in the early years of my relationship with Paul. One of the more touching, especially these days, happened around a particular scarf that I still wear to do this day during the Christmas season.

It was back in the early 1980s and the two of us were, frankly, poor. Both in grad school, both working full time, but at jobs that were just barely lucrative enough to cover our monthly expenses, living in a small rent-controlled apartment on the north side of Berkeley in the high-cost-of-living-even-then San Francisco Bay Area. Thus, when it came to the romantic gesture, our financial situation pretty much limited us to the kind of thing that could be carried off on a student's budget—discount red roses from the supermarket (which he strewed over the white bedspread one Valentine's Day rather theatrically—lovely but quite impractical, it took weeks to get the stains out) or a simple homemade picnic basket on a hike in the hills where all it cost us was the time to make sandwiches and a bit of inexpensive wine. Without funds, we found ourselves constrained to make up the difference with a bit more creativity as young lovers—not a bad thing at all, I might say, as I look back on that time in my life, especially now that he is gone, though often having a little bit more money at one's disposal can make many things much easier in all areas, especially gift-giving.

Between the two of us, I was definitely the more frugal and planful and he definitely much more the spendthrift and impulsive, but, as anyone who knew us would say, we both liked nice things. We'd grown up wanting for very little, had lived in Europe and Canada, respectively, and enjoyed the sensual and aesthetic beauty of good food, good design, tasteful clothes. Paul's father, a bit of a dandy himself, as it turned out, used to say that Paul had "champagne tastes on a beer budget," and that was literally true during our grad school years—and even good beer was a bit of a financial stretch at times. So, when the iconic luxury department store Neiman Marcus decided to open in San Francisco, with a glorious, crystal dome emporium designed by architect Philip Johnson, of course the two of us went that fall.

And I will say the store lived up to all its expectations (and still does): it was quite dazzling. So, the two of us had a bit of fun in it that day, as one might expect. I remember actually spending time trying on men's fur coats because, yes, there was actually an entire section of the fur coat section devoted exclusively to men's furs, and the gorgeous honey-colored sheared beaver jacket that I tried on that day even now remains burned in my sensual memory. Paul was a bit of a jewelry nut, had designed a beautiful gold ring for himself with religious imagery that he had made for himself in Milwaukee, a ring that we ended up making an identical copy of for our wedding three decades later, and he had always been entranced with the beauty of gemstones and beads. So we played a bit that day trying on coats, heats, rings, bracelets, necklaces, having a grand time.

Sometime during our afternoon there, before we went up to the glorious cupola restaurant and looked at the menu we couldn't afford, I took a detour through the colognes where Paul did not follow because of what I guess these days we call "chemical sensitivity." Never big on artificial scent—scented oils, perfumes, colognes, scented products, fragrant candles—I left him behind to explore the testers, and I eventually wandered through the women's accessories, where I had a bit of private fun looking at trying out scarves. A couple of scarves that I saw were especially beautiful, particularly the silk ones, because I already had appropriated quite a few of my own father's silk scarves from the 1940's and 1950s, and it was somewhat of a fashion "thing" for me back then—long wool coat, silk scarf, 1950s fedora, a little more suited to a colder East Coast winter than the much milder West Coast, but nevertheless, there were a couple of items I definitely would have bought if I had had the scratch. But I didn't, so off I went, met Paul up at the cupola, sprung for the cheapest thing we could buy, a cup of coffee and we called it a day at Neiman Markup, as it became humorously known around town.

It was only a couple of months later at Christmas, when to my surprise, Paul presents me with a Neiman Marcus box. Of course, I'm thrilled but also thinking to myself, whatever did he get me there? Whatever could he afford? And I was quite taken back to find that he had actually gotten me one of the scarves I had seen that day when we had gone—a beautiful long golden scarf in silk charmeuse with hand-painted cherubs on it and the words "angels are hovering around us."

"How did you know I had seen this at Nieman?" I asked. "That's crazy."

"I didn't, actually. I went back this past week without you, applied for a charge account there, which they gave me, and frankly maxed it out on this scarf which I just thought you would really like. It was hanging out near the aisle, the angels caught my eye, and it just seemed really Christmassy and kinda you."

Very unexpected and very synchronistic, this scarf remains to this day a cherished possession of mine which I now, almost ritually, bring out and wear exclusively during the Christmas season, and the story of it is always fun to tell.

But of course, as I tell this story, I've heard a few other such stories, even more synchronistic from friends, clients, readers and other who attend my talks and workshops. Suzanne's story of the pearl has quite a few parallel to my own.

"So, this story about my husband Cliff happened quite a while ago. I had just begun med school at the time and, as these things happen, the summer before I was going to be picking my whole life and moving it out here, that's when I had met him. Great guy, friend of friends back East, but I'm on track to start the craziness of full-on med school. He, however, fortuitously was between jobs, really didn't have a whole lot tying him to Massachusetts at the time, and in fact was somewhat eager to get away from the family, so even though we had only known one another a couple of months really, he followed me out and signed up for being my live-in boyfriend—unenviable, I still don't know many men who'd do that.

"Anyway, the relationship's new, and I'm pulling crazy shifts through all my rotations, but things are really good between us. He managed to find a job pretty quickly, not his dream job, but OK enough, and my whole recollection of that period—which had to be insane—is truthfully very romantic. Cliff is a *very* romantic guy, very family-oriented, he's the yin, and I'm definitely the yang between the two of us, so in that first year of tumultuous transition for both of us, I'm slowly getting to know him and to really fall deeply in love with him—his sensitivity, his support for me, his openness. I began to feel really, really fortunate, I still feel that way, because there aren't a lot of guys like him.

"So, where the hospital is where I'm assigned is up the hill a little from Clement Street which back then was a little Chinatown—lots of Chinese restaurants, shops, bookstores, very lively, busy. It's still like that a little only back then it was more so. But it's literally across town from where we're living, and now and then, when I get a break, I wander down there, sometimes for lunch, sometimes just to clear my head. And along Clement there are a couple of jewelry stores. Now, as you might expect, I'm not a big jewelry person. Not the most feminine chick, to start with, little tomboy, and trying to hold my own in a very male-dominated field that I'm going into, but from when I was little I sort of had this thing about pearls. My grandmother had a really beautiful pearl necklace that always fascinated me, with a pair of matching pearl-drop earrings, and I remember when she told me how pearls were made, I thought she was making it up until I looked it up in the encyclopedia and realized that, yes, they really did come from fish shells, at which point every time the family would go out to a fish restaurant., I'd be looking in my clams, mussels and oysters for a pearl.

"But it wasn't just that they were beautiful. In talking to my grandma about her pearls, I found out that there were a bunch of strange little superstitions about them, which when I was still a little girl made them even more mysterious. One Christmas, I think, it might have been a cousin of ours, maybe...anyway, someone in the family gave someone else pearls as a Christmas gift, and my grandma off to the side said to me, "Never give pearls as a gift. Pearls are tears." And I guess maybe the look on my face might have made her realize that she hadn't really been thinking about what she said, or that maybe I'd say something to this cousin who had gotten them, which would be pretty awkward, or maybe I brought up the fact that my grandfather had given her the pearls she always wore—I suspect that I might have said something like that because that's the kind of little girl I was back even then, so if they were tears, why would grandpa want to give her tears. Anyway, for whatever reasons, she went on to say, "unless you get them from your one true love, and then they will be tears of happiness." So that sealed the deal for me and the pearl thing. I was already fascinated by them but now they had this additional bit of magical, superstitious mojo behind them, too.

"In any case, literally the last thing any guy I had ever dated through high school and college would have ever thought of giving me was pearls, even though in my little secret heart of hearts, that's one of the things I really would have wanted. I got practical, science-oriented gifts—experiment kits, tools—because, well, that's just who I am. But there I am on Clement Street in medical school, looking in the jewelry shop windows and looking at the pearls, because by then, you know, those perfectly round, cultured pearls of my grandmother's time weren't the only kind of pearls you could get. In fact, I found myself much more drawn to the unique and fantastically shaped irregular fresh-water pearls, which were a little more my style anyway: when was a female doctor in the 1990s ever going to wear a big long strand of cultured pearls? But these Chinese shops had these very striking-looking pendants that I thought were quite something, large odd-shaped pearls set into a gold frame, just one, as a pendant, simple, beautiful, something I could actually see myself loving and wearing. And there were quite a few times I came this close to going into one of the shops and buying one of these for myself. Very close.

"So, my birthday comes around that spring, which means that Cliff and I have been with one another for almost a year and living together for a rather bumpy six months. Things are good for the most part, but it's really the first serious relationship for the two of us, definitely the first time either of us has lived with someone else, and well, there we are, frankly, still getting to know one another, when he hands me my birthday gift, my first birthday gift from him, by the way, and what is it but one of those gold-inset irregular pearls that I had been lusting after. There is absolutely no way he could have known about my private window-shopping, we didn't live anywhere near Clement Street, and while I might have mentioned my grandma's pearls to him in passing, I know I didn't go into all the superstitious lore about them she had had, nor would I have ever admitted wanting something so femmy in the jewelry line. But somehow, he knew and there it was, this really beautiful pearl pendant that I still have, a gift that did literally give me tears of happiness from my one true love.

"I absolutely grilled him on it, because the coincidence of it all was so weird, you know, but he didn't really cop to anything other than seeing them in the store one day and thinking how pretty they'd look, especially since they were fairly simple but still elegant, which struck him as my sort of style. He already knew I wouldn't want anything too frou-frou. And since then, the pearl thing has become a bit of a tradition with us—always a single freshwater irregular pearl, just one, sometimes a plain setting, sometimes a little more elaborate, and not every year, but I'd say I have now maybe six or seven pearl pendants from him on various occasions, and the first one he gave me is the one I wore at our wedding. It's become a bit of a signature, so to speak, and it means a lot to me."

These sorts of synchronistic events I tend to call "confirmatory" coincidences because, above and beyond the delightful nature of the surprise around which they occur, particular early on in the relationship, they have the effect of confirming the rightness of being together for the two people involved. Through them, it feels as if our partner "knows" us on a deep level, and so, I believe, they do. However, what I think the kind of knowledge that these synchronistic events bring to our attention is the unconscious knowledge of one another that lies at the heart of genuine love. Certainly, it would be a sign of thoughtfulness and caring attention to get me the scarf you had seen me admiring or the pendant I had heard you talk about now and then in passing. However, that these gifts were given coincidentally, though, raises our awareness—as synchronistic events are wont to do—of the wider and deeper field of unconscious attunement between the two people that grows over time and with experience. The depth of this attunement is disclosed in the synchronistic event that, in its turn, discloses the depth of the bond to us consciously. The brightness of this coming to consciousness constitutes the spontaneous wonder we feel, the cosmic delight, when such meaningful coincidences occur.

Since so much of our reflection in this chapter circles about time, it is especially intriguing to note a similar set of confirmatory synchronicities between couples arises from rather striking and entirely coincidental times and dates two people in love begin to discover that they share with one another. My friends Norma and Bill tell the story of moving forward in their commitment to one another by getting married, and picking a date in the middle of the summer. "We did that in part because my birthday is in the springtime and his is near Christmas, so it wasn't just to be sure of great weather but we intentionally thought about giving ourselves as a couple something to celebrate through the year, in every season. Now, I actually wanted to get married on August 15, because I had gone to a parochial school named Our Lady of the Assumption and my grandmother was named

Asunción, so that particular feast day was always very meaningful to me, but in the end, the priest dissuaded us from doing that, simply out of Catholic tradition. It is, he said, a little inappropriate to obscure a Marian feast day with one's own celebration, so he suggested that we do it the day after, August 16, and that if I wanted to think of our wedding as simply part of the octave of the Feast of the Assumption, that would be one way to ask for Our Lady's blessing. So that's what we did, and it was a beautiful wedding, a lovely Mass. But it was only afterward that Bill and I found out about two very synchronistic things about that date. The first, something that I didn't know at all, came through my cousin the week afterward. She and I were going through the wedding gifts and she said, 'Norma, you know, don't you that your grandma Asunción died on August 16,' which in fact I did not know. She died when I was little and in the Philippines, and I think I only met her once. 'Yes,' said my cousin, 'we all thought it was very funny how she was named Asunción and had always had such a devotion to the Blessed Mother. It was almost as if Mary had gone to heaven the day before and opened heaven to her.' I was very surprised as you can imagine, and my cousin was surprised that I was surprised. 'So, you didn't pick the date August 16 for her?' And I explained that no, we didn't, we actually wanted August 15, the feast day, but were told we shouldn't. Like most of us Filipinos, my cousin believes in all these spiritual connections and, she said to me, 'So the mistake wasn't a mistake, maybe, huh?' And yes, it did feel, when I found that out, like my grandma was in a way there at our wedding blessing us behind the scenes, and I liked how my wedding anniversary would now forever be a way to remember her and ask her to help us as a couple.

"But the really strange thing is that it does not end there. It was a quite a few years later, my husband Bill started doing genealogy research on his family, and when we traveled to Ireland, on vacation really, he decided to see if he could do a little digging on his relatives there. So, we go to the town that his mother's family came from, where in fact his grandmother was born, and what do we find out but that his grandmother's birthday actually was not the day he thought it was, the day that they all used to celebrate it, August 17, but it was actually recorded in the church's birth records as August 16. The two of us really couldn't believe first that the whole family had been celebrating her birthday on the wrong day—I still cannot figure out how you get someone's birthday wrong, but that side of his family has a lot of problems, so let's leave it at that. But more personally, it was just the strangest thing to see the actual birth date as August 16, which is the day my grandmother died and the day we ourselves chose to get married. It was like a weird coming together of dates and times and births and deaths, you know. And it makes our anniversary every year even more special."

Here, again, is the way in which these stories throw yet another light on the nature of our subjective experience of time, as this sort of confluence of dates and times becomes a synchronistic element wherein chronological time intersects with the events in our lives and relationships to confirm and to heighten our awareness of the significance of our family relationships. In Norma's story, it would be one thing for them to have intentionally chosen that particular date as a way to knit together past, present, and future, their maternal ancestors with their spiritual mother Mary, on the day of their wedding, but in their case it happened purely by chance.

Another such story of chronology synchronistically emphasizing the family's unity and relatedness comes from Devon who told me that, while he was aware he and his eventual wife Linda had gone on their first date on October 10, 2010—which was his mother's birthday—what they could not of course know at the time was that their first daughter would be born one year and a day later, on October 11, 2011, and that his wife Linda's sister's first baby would be born the following year on October 12, 2012. Now I do hear about these kinds of meaningful coincidences a fair bit, and I have a fair bit of experience with them myself in my own life between me and my family members and even some friends. But I like to push a bit when people tell me their stories— it's the psychotherapist in me that wants to go a little deeper. So, when Devon told me about all of his intersecting dates, I asked him what he made of it, because after all, that's the answer which goes to the heart of the synchronicity—what do you make of the coincidence?

He raised his eyebrows a little, not expecting the question. "Hmm, I don't know what to make of it. It's the kind of thing we're obviously not planning, but if I was just going to talk off the top of my head, what I would say is that it gives me a sense of time marching on. 10-10-10. 10-11-11. 10-12-12. It's like the dates are a bit of a tick-tock-tick-tock, especially when you factor the kids into it, which I would say represent our future. Little did Linda and I know back on October 10, 2010 what we were starting."

What I believe goes without saying in all of the above, and what, for example, Devon's off-the-cuff interpretation of these calendrical synchronicities has front and center, is one of those essential characte-ristic of synchronicity that I discussed in the introduction: the symbolic nature of the event. Now of course, when it comes to something like the material object—the scarf I was given or the pearl pendants which slowly evolved into a family tradition between Suzanne and her husband—the symbolic nature of the gift is hard to ignore. The act of giving itself, of course, is its own symbol: of love, of generosity of heart, of thoughtfulness, of a selflessness that represents what the intimacy of our relationship essentially incarnates. But the very gift itself, in all its physical reality, has a deep symbolic resonance as well. The scarf shines with the golden brilliance of the feeling we share and I wrap myself up with it as I feel my soul wrapped in the warmth and beauty of my beloved. The pearls Suzanne was given have, each one of them, the unique and lustrous one-of-a-kind shape that represents the singularity of her marriage with Cliff, and if pearls are tears, then that, too, is what Suzanne now wears when she places the pendant around her neck, a symbol of the joy and the sadness that comes together in one single spot of beauty.

But in a way, I find Norma's and Devon's stories even more evocative because they disclose yet another aspect of what one of my themes for this discussion has been, the nature of time: namely, how one experience we have of time which we might think of as consummately ordinary and prosaic—the lowly date on a calendar, the number of the day, month or year—actually can acquire through synchronistic experiences a richly symbolic meaning for ourselves and our families. To anyone raised in an observant religious tradition, the sacred nature of calendar time will hardly be a surprise, for there is no spiritual tradition of depth that does not mark time with a special care in reference to the fundamental truths and events from within that tradition. But what I think these stories of synchronistic experiences between couples and family members brings to our attention, is that there is a similar process of marking off sacred time from within the smaller communities of our families that arises from our own subjective experience of connection between ourselves and those we love. Just as there is a parallel between the larger myths of creation as told by a whole culture and the smaller myths of origin told by couples at the start of a family tradition, so, too, we see a parallel between larger religious traditions holding chronological time symbolically and smaller family traditions of how chronological time—the days and the years—reflects what we mean to one another and how we are connected. Norma's story, in a way does both, since her own family's story is a deeply symbolic intersection of religious imagery around the Virgin Mary, evoking the broader Catholic tradition of her family, punctuated by the feast days and the sacrament of marriage, and the somewhat surprisingly dense complex of special days particular to her family's birthdays and anniversaries, unexpectedly reaching across generations. It is this forward motion of time that Devon, too, perceived when I pushed him a bit to make his own interpretation of the synchronistic complex of dates he told me about: as he put it, tick-tock, tick-tock, the meaning of the birthdays and anniversaries slowly became layered with more meaning as the past became present flowing into the future.

What I believe both types of these stories of synchronistic meetings make explicit, whether they are synchronicities of circumstance or synchronicities of commonality, is that time is not just a physical reality nor an arbitrary construct, but indeed a multi-faceted archetypal reality which we encounter precisely in the events of our own history, and nowhere in our lives does our own history come alive more vividly and more consistently than in our families. And in a way these personal myths of origin we all have within our families take on their power for us as stories because of the wonder of coincidence that stands behind them, and the great coming together of two people that they represent. Hardly surprising, I would say, that such stories show us this special relationship between love, history, and our inner archetypal reality: as a principle of connection, synchronicity seems an apt phenomenon within the realm of relationship, and there is always a natural delight in connecting, in the deep sharing of our lives with those we love. But beyond how good it feels and how right it is to find and create a life with those we love, these stories also tell how our wholeness as people comes from such connections, these bonds of love. Our families, the families we come from and the families we create, represent one manner of wholeness we experience in our life as human beings, literally, to be sure, but perhaps even more importantly, symbolically and everlastingly.

CHAPTER THREE
Sharing the Present--Synchronicity and Siblings

I met Kathleen for a coffee downstairs from my office on a bright spring morning. "I haven't told my story to many people, for a couple of reasons," she said to me. "Mostly, I would say, besides being a somewhat private person, there's a way in which what I share with my sister is something the two of us actually like to keep between us, a bit like our special secret. And of course—maybe this is my own projection—I think at times that people won't really believe it." She pulled out a small notebook and showed it to me. "Until Donald said to me that you were writing this book and urged me to talk to you, I hadn't really sat down and, you know, intentionally gone through the various things Danielle and I have experienced together, and of course as I went through in my mind the details of some of the classic incidents between us, I remembered more things, somewhat subtle things, maybe they are synchronistic, maybe they are just the normal things two sisters share, I don't know. You're the expert." She laughed.

I shrugged at that, as I usually do, when people are telling me their stories about meaningful coincidences. "Actually, you're the expert on your own experience. If it's meaningful to you, I want to hear about it."

"I appreciate that," she said. "In going through it all, I thought the best place to start would be at the beginning, but that's a little hard to explain, because I would say that what I call my psychic connection to Danielle was something that didn't appear suddenly or dramatically, but was a kind of awareness that I only gradually as a young child became aware of. I'm three years older than she is, and I definitely remember my mother being pregnant with her, even at that early age, and I had a great deal of excitement, like most little kids I would imagine, about having a baby sister. Which was, according to my mother, perhaps the first sign. I was *convinced* it was going to be a girl, and you see how old I am, this was at a time and a place when it wasn't common or even possible to figure out the baby's sex beforehand. My mother, when she was alive, often talked about how dead certain I was that the new baby was going to be a girl, to the point that she actually was a little worried what would happen for me if it ended up being a boy, so she said she would try to talk to me about that. 'Kathleen, honey, you know, you may have a baby brother,' and she said that I would just look at her and shake my head and smile. 'Mommy, it's a baby sister. My baby sister.'

"And, of course, I was right," Kathleen chuckled. "Given that I had a good 50-50 chance of being right, so I don't know how amazing that was, or if that even qualifies as synchronistic or psychic, but I'm telling you this because for me, that I knew she was a girl was always, for me, a bit of a sign that I had a connection to Danielle even then, a connection that goes back before she was born, so her birth was quite a memorable event for me even at age 3. I remember my mother going into labor, I remember my aunt coming to stay with me that night, the whole event really sticks out in my mind. And Danielle came very quickly into the world, within a few hours of the start of labor—which is a detail, again, that this part of the family story, especially because of my sister's personality. She's quite the lively go-getter, very physically active, very dynamic, and in that way a bit of a contrast to me, who is a good deal quieter, reflective, cautious. Very different personalities.

"Now I can't say I remember Danielle coming home precisely but there is a very specific memory I have of being with her." Kathleen closed her eyes, envisioning the scene. "I'm standing on some kind of step stool next to her crib, so that I'm tall enough to look over, and I can see here wrapped in a blanket, her little round face and blue eyes peeking out, and there is this moment in which she and I look at each other. It was for me a bonding moment, now that I have had my own kids, I know there's that one moment when you first really *see* this new human being that you are going to be connected to for the rest of your life, and that was the moment I remember with Danielle in her crib. And I may be reading back into the situation, but the two thoughts I had then, the two thoughts that I have always felt with regard to my sister, were: I am not alone anymore, that is to say, I have a life companion now, and the second thought was less a thought and more of a feeling, a very strong protective feeling toward her, like it was my job in life to make sure she would be OK. So companionship and protection."

Kathleen looked down at her journal that she had brought with her to our meeting, read a bit and then looked up again. "So, as I was going over this story for you, I felt like those two things were important because in a way all of the rest of it grows out of that for me. Sometime in the first couple of years together, I look back and I realize that I was very tuned in, I would say, to Danielle. My mother noticed it and often joked when she was still alive about how much of a 'little mama' I was back then, in a strange way, telling her what Danielle wanted or coming to her and saying things about what she liked or didn't like. Everyone, of course, thought it was very cute, and I will admit I don't really have specific memories of this or that, but what is true and what I did have a sense of throughout was a kind of connection or awareness of what was going on with her. My mother said I'd sometimes be sitting in the living room and just very matter-of-factly tell her that Danielle was waking up and was going to be hungry, and a few minutes later, sure enough, she'd start crying in the other room for her bottle. A couple of times I'd tell my mother she was cold or hot, and once again, after checking on the baby, my mother found she was uncovered or not bundled enough. As I said, those are a bit of family lore and I myself don't have a specific memory of doing things like that, but I don't really have any reason to think my parents would make something like that up.

"Anyway, the first time I myself became aware that there was more of a connection than could be easily explained was once I went to school. I think a lot of the stories my mother tells about my connection to Danielle can in fact be explained away by my being perhaps a very intuitive child sharing a relatively small house with a new baby that I'm intensely focused on. I'm sure there are all kinds of maybe subliminal noises, subtle sounds or smells, you know, things like that which little kids are very sensitive to, but once I go to kindergarten, where I'm at school and the baby is at home, that's when for the first time it got, shall I say, more interesting.

"There was this one afternoon, we had a kind of a nap time around that time of day, we'd all bring out these little mats, and have some kind of snack, milk, graham crackers, and settle down for what was probably only a few minutes but it seemed like a big long siesta to us, of course. I'm sure it was mostly to give the teacher a break from a classroom of crazy five-year-olds for a moment or two. We'd draw the blinds, and everyone would then 'practice being quiet.' I always thought that was a funny phrase, and I used it with my own kids growing up. Anyway, it was during that naptime one day that I became aware, I don't know how to say it, that something was just not right with Danielle.

"Now over the years, I've spoken to a few people about their psychic experiences and read plenty of books. I guess some people actually share the physical experiences of others, family members, twins, siblings, whatever. That's never been the case with me, I've never actually physically shared the experience, you know, felt in my own body what she was feeling, but there is, I don't know how to describe it, a certain kind of inner *knowing*. It is very solid and very sure, and it usually has this edge of anxiety or fear to it. There's also usually a sense of urgency, and it's quite striking because it often comes out of nowhere and especially at quiet times. So that day, in the middle of my naptime, as a kindergartener, I'm wide awake and go up to the teacher and tell her that I need to go home right now, my sister is sick.

"Well, you can imagine, the teacher's response to that because after all it wasn't that uncommon occurrence for a parade of itchy and overactive five-year-olds to make stuff up in the middle of an enforced naptime. She was sweet but obviously skeptical, and even though I was insistent, I was sent back to my mat. But the whole rest of the afternoon, which was in reality just a couple of hours, I was very unhappy and felt like I couldn't wait to get back home.

"Sure enough, that day, my mother isn't the one to come pick me up, but *very* unusually, my dad who commuted into an office almost an hour away, so for him to be showing up at my elementary school at three o'clock in the afternoon was totally strange, and the moment I get in the car, he says that Mom is at the hospital with Danielle who is being treated for an acute ear infection. Again, I don't remember this myself but part of the family story, according to him, is that on hearing that news, I said to him, 'I told my teacher that I needed to go home because Danielle was sick but she wouldn't believe me.'

"Again, was that chance? Was that intuition? I can tell you, whatever it was, that was when I realized for myself, and I'm just speaking for myself now, that there was more of a connection between her and me than could be easily understood by most people, including myself, and that was the moment when, in a way, I simply accepted it as an emotional fact. It wasn't until much later that I spoke about it, because I think even as a child I realized that my experiences wouldn't be taken seriously, but that first time when I was in kindergarten and she had an ear infection was when I became aware of the connection for myself.

"So, this sort of thing continued throughout our childhood, this weird sort of second-sense of where she was, what she was doing, whether or not she needed help or assistance. There was a time when I was maybe around ten and she was seven or eight, and somehow she had gotten stuck up in a tree she had climbed into, in our backyard, and I was playing down the street, inside, at the house of other friends, absolutely no way to know what was happening, and boom, somehow, this inner certainty and urgency hit me, at which point, I stop playing, get up, and go home and find her sitting up there in the tree, frustrated and even a little scared, not knowing how to get down. There were a number of incidents like that as kids between her and me, mostly because, as I said, she was quite the tomboy and always getting into things. She smashed her knee once down the street skateboarding with the neighborhood boys, and I was reading in my bedroom and again somehow *knew* something had happened. I went to my mother who was ironing and told her to turn off the iron because she was going to have to take Danielle to the doctor, just minutes before Danielle walked in with this bloody mess on her leg. That happened a couple of times, things like that, when I somehow knew about an illness or injury of hers somewhat telepathically."

Kathleen paused for a moment. "So, there are a couple of things about all of this which are a little interesting to me. The first is that these incidents are all one-way. I'm very aware of Danielle, but if you speak to her, she doesn't have a similar psychic connection to me. Next is that my own daughter has this kind of connection with me. She has at times had an intuitive and psychic sense of my states or things that are happening with me from a distance, but as far as my sister Danielle, I'm the one who has this kind of connection to her, but it's not reciprocal. And another thing about it all which I also find interesting is that my connection is almost exclusively about her physical well-being. I don't really have a sense of her emotional states from a distance. A few years back, she had a family crisis that was mostly emotional in nature—found out her husband had been unfaithful, had all of the reactions you'd expect her to have—and I only found out about it weeks later. Not a big surprise to me, I never liked the guy to begin with. They eventually split up, which also I wasn't too broken up about, but the point is that at that time I had absolutely no sense that anything troubling was going on with her. But when she had her two kids, I knew when she went into labor, both times, in fact, the second time, really in a way just to make the point, I didn't even call her I just went to the hospital, fully prepared to have the staff tell me she wasn't there, but what actually happened was that she had just gotten there an hour before and was already in labor and delivery. Just a couple of years ago, I was at work and once again, boom, I get this feeling in the pit of my stomach, and so now with cell phones and texting and so forth, I can make immediate contact, and there it was, she had just been rear-ended and the impact had given her minor whiplash and literally a minute after it happened, I was calling her.

"Now, given that she has no experiences like this and has been on the receiving end of it, what she would probably say to you is that it's a little weird but also a little reassuring. And frankly, I myself think it's a little weird, but at this point it's just a feature of our relationship as sisters, this odd one-way synchronistic connection between us which has always been there for me."

In listening to Kathleen's story, obviously, the easiest thing would be to simply put down her experiences to what one commonly calls a "psychic connection" between two people, in this case, between her and her sister. Perhaps at one point in our culture, this sort of explanation for this rather dramatic, at times, and life-long series of perceptions might have been looked upon skeptically, and in some quarters, I'm sure it still is. But really since Rhine's experiments in the 1950s on ESP, which Jung himself discussed in his own work on synchronicity, my impression is that most people accept at least the possibility, if not the established reality, that certain individuals among us have a "sixth sense," the capacity to feel and know what is happening, as in Kathleen's case, to someone who is not physically present to them. I have heard enough stories over the course of my life and career to be fairly convinced that indeed, some people really do, to varying degrees, have a level of deep intuitive perception that manifests itself in ways we've come to call "psychic," and I myself have upon occasion had such telepathic flashes of experience or dreams, some of which I recounted in *There Are No Accidents* and that I have written about elsewhere, as they have manifested in my therapy work with certain clients.

So, going about the process of trying to understand or explain these experiences is quite natural, but what is also important to be clear about in this regard, in my opinion, and especially in relationship to the concept of synchronicity is that attributing these amazing connections between siblings, in this case, to a sixth sense or psychic abilities, is to adduce a causal explanation for these experiences. And frankly, I'm always a little amused, to be honest, at just how blithely, particularly these days, how many people "explain away" such events as "*just* another example of psychic perception" or "*just* my ESP at work again." I find it, first of all, highly ironic and indeed quite contradictory to affirm what is in fact a rather extraordinary phenomenon in human experience, as if it were proven reality, while simultaneously dismissing it as if it were a simple ordinary accepted reality. "Oh, that's *just* Kathleen being psychic," as if one heard a doorbell and said, "Oh, that's *just* someone at the door," or as if one walked into the house and smelled something baking and said, "Oh that's *just* my mother making lasagna." If certain among us have such psychic abilities and extrasensory perceptiveness, I think it bears stating that this is an extraordinary thing, a rare and rather wondrous phenomenon in human experience. Reducing it down to a normal everyday experience is to do this unusual aspect of our human capacities a grave disservice.

But more relevant to the topic of synchronicity is that such explanations for experiences such as Kathleen's are just that: explanations, that is to say, *causal* attributions of these circumstances to a sixth sense these individuals possessed. When it comes to the specifically synchronistic nature of such stories, I'd like us all to remember that such causes, even if true, really are actually irrelevant to what the events *mean* to Kathleen. And I, for one, find the meaning of the event, the emotional significance, the symbolic impact of these lifelong connections, far more interesting and compelling. In Kathleen's case, she told her story to me quite eloquently in such a way as to make this point clear: the psychic aspect of her connection, yes, was striking but they constituted just one part of an entire fabric of relationship she had with her sister that began even before her sister was born. What the details of the synchronistic events actually were have their place, but what they *meant* to her is what jumps out in the fuller story, how they stand as a characteristic of her relationship to her sister.

And in this regard, what Kathleen told me about her experience handily illustrates one of the basic points I feel such synchronistic family experiences make clear: that our family bonds are made, not given. Time after time, the powerful coincidence of an internal state of anxiety or concern, that Kathleen felt subjectively, meeting the external circumstance of what was happening at the same time in Danielle's life laid a foundation for the particular quality of Kathleen's emotional and symbolic tie to her sister. Over and over, these coincidences became Kathleen's story about how Danielle is a vital part of her life, not just by the simple virtue of being born from the same mother, but by what these coincidences *meant* to her.

All of which is illustrated even more sharply by the fact that these synchronistic events were, in Kathleen's case, one-way: she had the deep internal psychic connection to Danielle but Danielle, for her part, did not have the same for Kathleen. This may seem like a small detail but it goes to an important part of the concept of synchronicity as an acausal connecting principle. If a single event or series of events has a significance for one of the individuals participating and feels synchronistic while simultaneously, the very same event occurring to the very same person at the very same is just merely curious or surprising but devoid of any deep impact or abiding meaningfulness, then clearly the synchronicity is not in the event but within us. The meaning is not "out there," in the facts of the occurrence but, rather, "in here," in the world of our own interior psychological and emotional lives. Danielle is simply going about living her life, but Kathleen is the one experiencing an entirely other level of richness of connection when these events coincide, and it is the compendium of these experiences throughout her life that become fashioned into the story I was told about her sense of "sisterhood" with Danielle.

This is a truth about families that I talk about a great deal with my clients in the course of my family therapy work, and I generally find that stating this truth is both liberating and welcome. Stories of synchronicity between siblings like Kathleen's are one place we see this truth most clearly: we think of our family relationships as being a "given" but in fact, they aren't. Rather, they are *made*, slowly and carefully fashioned, usually unconsciously outside of awareness, and altogether spontaneously as we grow up beside the people we are born to and share our family with. Sometimes, I would say, ideally, the relationship that is fashioned is one of deep and loving connection, but sometimes, maybe even often, it is not, and especially when it is not— when there is estrangement, misunderstanding, even tragically hostility or abuse—that is when what Kathleen's story illustrates becomes even more important to remember, that our family relationships are *made*, not given. We do have choices about what sort of relationship we have with those to whom we are related, and the character of the bond we feel need not be purely unconscious and instinctive. Such synchronistic events between siblings, like the ones between Kathleen and Danielle, show us this truth. It is not merely what happened, but rather what we make of it that matters.

As has often occurred in my work around synchronicity, I have found when doing research about a specific topic there is often a "run" on the same kind of story or event. Bob, an acquaintance of mine from, of all places, my gym, when I mentioned that I was working on this, book told me a similar sort of story of sibling protectiveness, as it were—less explicitly psychic, I might say, and therefore, perhaps some-what more of an "ordinary" kind of synchronicity of the sort that might occur to any of us. But I found his story also quite instructive about the nature of synchronistic events and how they fit into what we make of our sibling relationships. As so it happened that while working out one day, he and I got to talking, and seeing as we were both two older guys doing our weight routine in the middle of the day, he asked if I was retired, too, to which I said I wasn't, but that I only saw clients two days a week and the other days, lately, I was devoting to a book on meaning-ful coincidences. Was it synchronistic for me that Bob actually had a story about synchronicity, and particularly about a sibling?

"That's such a funny thing to hear," he said, "because my brother and I have had a kind of a running joke, I guess you would say, between us, and it was something that we only really noticed after it happened a few times. These things run in series, don't they?"

It was my turn to laugh, because I had just gotten finished writing the section of this book in the introduction in which I address that. "As a matter of fact...."

"So, the first couple of times, I wouldn't say Kenny and I really paid much attention to it, and this was back when I was working in the city every day. You know how the traffic is, and of course I'm feeling like I'm spending half my life in the car, so a lot of times, what would happen is that if, for whatever reason, I wasn't able to get out of the house early enough to beat the traffic, I'd often just head over to BART, park and pop into the city that way. And, I don't know, with two teenagers and my wife's work schedule, and this and that which would always seem to happen just as I was about to leave the house, whether I was going in by car or going in by BART was pretty much a toss-up day to day.

"Anyway, the time when it came to my attention was actually one of those incidents that you find yourself getting really pissed off about. So, my brother Kenny is a bit of a Berkeley free spirit, professional musician, so he's up at all hours, composing, playing a gig, whatever, and it really wasn't at all uncommon for him to simply lose all track of time. When we were younger, the two of us, before cell phones made it even crazier, my wife Jan and I would sometimes hear the phone ring in the middle of the night, and you know how you do, you think the worst, only I knew it was probably Kenny not realizing it was 3 am, and there he is on the other end of the line wanting to talk about, who knows what, politics or something wild that happened to a neighbor of his. Anyway, these completely random phone calls of his at all hours were a very Kenny thing, and now with caller ID, I will say both Jan and I are much happier because back when, especially when the kids were small, the damn phone would ring in the middle of the night, the whole house would get woken up, it was not a good scene. But now, even though Kenny blocks his caller ID, I know it's him because he and my dentist's office are the only two 'private numbers' that ever call me.

"So, the first time I noticed what was happening with him and his damn phone calls was actually pretty dramatic. I'm getting my act together to get out of the house in the morning—and I'm thinking I'm doing pretty good—the kids were cooperating, Jan and I were clicking, and it's one of those mornings when you're like, 'It's going to be good day ahead,' and then, phone rings, and like an idiot I answer it, and it's Kenny, 'Hey bro, what's up? Say, I wanted to ask you....' and to tell you the truth, I actually don't even remember the specifics of the conversation, maybe he was asking to borrow the hedge clippers or going on about the election or whatever. With Kenny, it sorta didn't matter, but whatever it was that day, the time it took me to get him off the phone was just long enough to delay me and sure enough, I get on the freeway and it's a wall of traffic onto the bridge which is when I just cut and run and head over to the BART station.

"So, as it turns out that particular day, the traffic ended up being an all-day long nightmare because of a horrible multi-car and truck crash on the Bay Bridge which closed the whole span for most of the

114

morning and which, I realized later that day, when I watched the news, I probably would have been right in the middle of, had I not been delayed, and in fact, when I said that at dinner that night, I think Jan my wife pointed out that that was actually the third time that had happened to me, that a phone call from Kenny had delayed me and that that delay had actually taken enough time or re-routed me so as to avoid a traffic mess. The first time she reminded me of this, it actually had been the opposite of this one. It had been a time when I was already late and was heading to BART, and that was when Kenny called to tell me that BART was totally FUBAR, someone had fallen on the track at the transfer station and all the trains throughout the whole system were stopped, he had just seen it on the news. So that day, weirdly, because of his phone call, I hopped in my car and breezed into the city to work. I had forgotten all about it.

"And then Jan also reminded me of another time when I was supposed to go to San Rafael, north of the city, for a conference, and Kenny called in a huge panic about his water heater, and needed me to come over and help him relight it. So, I dashed over to his house to lend him a hand and that day, the normal freeway entrance I would take from our house in Oakland was the scene of a terrible collision, and if I hadn't gone over to Kenny's house in Berkeley first, I probably would have been literally trapped on our freeway on-ramp for an hour and definitely would have missed the morning session of the conference I was supposed to go. But because I was over at Kenny's, I got onto the freeway at a place farther up than I usually would have, missed the backup, not to mention traffic was actually therefore kind of light, and in the end, I got there in less time than it would have ordinarily taken me.

"So, this time was actually not the first time, but the *third* time, and I spent the day at work half-joking to my co-workers that maybe I should thank my clueless brother for his phone call, because he rescued me from being in the middle of the Bay Bridge mess. However, when

Jan reminded me of the other ones, the previous two times that the same sort of thing happened, I got a little bit of gooseflesh, you know?

"And that's what the really strange thing is about it, I have to say, because it's totally not like Kenny is over there watching the traffic news for me and calling me up because he's using an app and telling me how to get where I'm going. He's really, God bless him, in his own world, and that was always a *huge* source of tension between the two of us. That was the sibling rivalry. He was the older one who more or less got away with whatever he wanted to do, the free spirit, as I said, the artistic one that my parents in a way indulged and gave all kinds of leeway, and I think, in reaction, maybe to differentiate myself, I decided to go the opposite route, Mr. Responsibility, self-discipline, order, always have my homework done and organized, room clean, everything in its place, clothes folded and hung up, which really made Kenny look worse, or so I thought in my eyes. I was definitely the younger sib trying to curry favor and to some extent it worked. I mean, my parents didn't ever complain about me or have to bail me out or make excuses for my behavior, whereas that was pretty much par for the course around Life with Kenny growing up. And we followed that pattern right into adulthood. I met my wife in college, and we've been together now 35 years. I'm at the same job, she at the same school, totally Mr. Stability—but with this crazy-assed older brother who in fact is living in my parents' house, because this and that music gig is barely enough, and still needs a bunch of help to keep himself together.

"Anyway, from that day forward, after Jan pointed it out, we began noticing in fact that it has happened a couple of times more since. You may or may not remember that enormous paint truck spill that happened on 580 a couple of years ago? Well, that was another situation in which, had everything gone according to my plan that day, I probably once again would have been completely stuck in a parking lot on the freeway behind it, because it happened right at the start of rush hour and I would have absolutely been right there, *except* that day Kenny called, and when I look at my wife to say it was Kenny, she gave me one of those looks like, you know, cocked her head as if to say, 'pay attention, Bob!' So that day, instead of rushing him off the phone, which is what I usually would do, I actually *intentionally* let him blather on— not an easy thing for me to do, let me tell you after a lifetime of being annoyed at him, and wouldn't you know, by the time I got in the car to go, the accident was all over the news and every traffic report was avoid 580 at all costs.

"So, I do hate to say this, but I now actually wonder when Kenny is calling in the morning whether or not he's saving me from traffic disaster. But of course, the weirdest thing of all is that he really doesn't know anything about it. I just cannot bring myself to tell him that his crazy phone calls have often saved my butt. I really cannot give him the satisfaction of knowing that," Bob laughed out loud. "Does that make me a bad person? I mean, I just cannot sit down and say, 'thanks, Kenny, but because you are a disorganized, chaotic loony bird that disrupts my life, you've helped me get to my job on time more often than you know.' I just can't!"

There are certain features of Bob's story in common with Kathleen's, specifically the way in which—though obviously both siblings are engaged in a single event—the synchronistic aspect of it, the meaning of it, comes home only to one of them, while the other is in a way an unwitting participant. In other words, another example of how the meaning is not *out there* in the raw facts but rather *in us* by what we make of it. Bob's story makes this point even clearer, though. Kathleen's emotional closeness to her sister might tempt us to think that the significance of their shared experiences grew out of that closeness and intimacy, whereas with Bob and Kenny a similar pattern of one-sided synchronistic experience but within the context of a relationship between two brothers which, though clearly affectionate, was nevertheless, at least explicitly for Bob, somewhat contentious and even at time downright annoying. Our family connections may have all manner of emotional valences to them—loving, competitive, sweet, clueless, annoying, comforting—and yet regardless of the tone or character, it may take a synchronistic event to bring us to consciousness about what we share.

Moreover, Bob's is the kind of a synchronicity story I cherish because, unlike perhaps many readers of this book who are intrigued by synchronistic events and are actively seeking out such experiences, his family story about his brother demonstrates how you can even be resistant to finding such connections or acknowledging the impact of them in one's life and still they happen. In his case, somewhat humorously, it took Bob's wife to point out the whole series of unintentional coincidences between him and his brother, and if I bring my family-therapist perspective to bear on this detail, I might be inclined to say that was because of the sibling rivalry between the two of them since childhood. Did Bob's disdain for his brother's disorganized personal style, his determination to be different, his little-brother position in the birth order blind him, or we would say, "keep him unconscious, lead him to repress the contribution those very aspects of his older brother Kenny's personality were making to his life, until they became literal and concrete in a repeatedly synchronistic way?"

Were Bob a client of mine, this area of his unconsciousness is what I would wish to explore with him in session: here we have at least five specific incidents in which the very thing you find the most annoying about your brother ends up being—by complete chance—the factor which, rather than disrupting your life, instead facilitates and assists you in going where you want to go and being whom you want to be, that prompt, organized, skillful person in the world. This is an insight that I've found at the heart of my counseling with couples or families: how the so-called "presenting problem"—that aspect of a family member or spouse's personality which the client complains the most vociferously about—is often underneath it all, in a quite ironic way, the very aspect of their personality which challenges the client to grow in ways they need to grow. And building upon the notion that our family relationships are not just simply given unconsciously but are best consciously fashioned, I then sometimes go so far as to suggest to the client, as I probably would to a client like Bob, that his brother's shadow side is something he may actually wish to consider embracing and even integrating into his own personality. After all, he's now had a whole series of experiences in which his brother's spontaneity ended up, quite synchronistically, helping him out. Indeed, as Bob admitted, it did take his wife to point this out, but as a therapist I can say that this is often the case and almost always the role I play. In fact, it's quite human: we sometimes require that someone else invite us outside our everyday consciousness and take a minute to reflect and to appreciate.

And Bob and Kenny show us also that it's an ambivalent bond, we have with our brothers and sisters. Our differences simultaneously separate us and bring us into relationship with one another, and whether the synchronistic events are rich with conscious affection and connection, as with Kathleen, or somewhat surprising and unbidden, as with Bob, we find ourselves navigating that ambivalence with our siblings throughout our lives.

Now, Quentin had come into psychotherapy with me a number of years before I heard this story, and like a lot of my clients, the original presenting problem—anxiety and work stress—was something we were able to pretty solidly resolve within the first year or so of our work, and that's usually a point in the course of psychotherapy when the client has a bit of a decision to make. Do we continue our work together and dive more deeply and fully into exploring their interior life as they go about the daily activities of work, relationships, friendships, and family—that is, set aside our regular weekly therapy hour as a space to reflect, to consider, to make connections, to look underneath—or do we shake hands and say, "glad that problem got resolved, glad you are feeling better, go forth and live happily," bringing our therapy work to a conclusion, at least until there's another situation or crisis or difficulty for which my support and insight might be needed or helpful? As I tell my interns, when I reach this point with clients, it's pretty 50-50: about 50 percent of them stay, continue in psychotherapy and use our relationship as a place for inward exploration, not because they need to any longer, but because they want to, consciously and deliberately, unhampered by any significant difficulties in their outer lives. The other 50 percent, sometimes due to a more practical bent of personality or because of limited time or financial resources, choose instead to bring the work to a close once the original presenting problem is resolved. Neither choice is right or wrong, of course, but in Quentin's case, he continued past the resolution of his initial concerns and had come to use our weekly sessions very productively, in my opinion. In particular, he was specifically intrigued by dream work, and how the imagery of his nightly dreams provided him with a sometime very startling and counter-intuitive perception of outer events. Quentin was definitely a client who didn't *need* to be in psychotherapy but rather *enjoyed* having the space and time to devote to his inner development.

It was in the course of discussing a dream with him then, some years into our work together, that he finally told me about this synchronistic aspect of his childhood which I had never before heard. The dream was a simple one, and as I sometimes say when running dream workshops or trainings, the simplest dreams can often unlock months and months of material for exploration, while the highly complicated, multi-episodic ones often are so confused and confusing that they are useless, going into too many directions at once to get our minds around what they might mean. However, Quentin's dream was decidedly spare in its imagery, as he first reported it to me, and indeed was nothing more than a photograph of a young child that he was holding in his hand, at which point he realized the photograph was actually alive, and the boy in it looked at Quentin, smiled and simply said, "Hello, again."

At first glance, it might seem like there's not much there to discuss, but I've learned never underestimate the depth and complexity of even a single inner image. I had a client once who dreamt of a single number—this was the number of the house she grew up in, except the four digits were reversed—and we literally discussed that dream for months and month, for that number, each of its digits, and its reversal in the dream had far-ranging, indeed, nearly endless connections, associations and meanings for her, in her history and with various symbolic implications. That's when I came to appreciate the hidden density of our inner symbolic life and how a simple surface of a single image can be the visible tip of a vast profusion of meaning.

Those were my initial thoughts about Quentin's talking photograph, when he told me the dream: holding the picture, in his hand, in semi-darkness, a young child, and not just "hello" but "hello, again." It was this last detail that intrigued me the most. In doing dream work with clients, I like to pay attention to what aspect of the dream seems to have the most "juice" for me as I listen to it—what catches my attention, what seems out of place, the most mysterious or uncanny, what detail poses a question or provides an answer or is unexpected? "Again"? It was that "again" at the end which made me pause and think, so while I let Quentin get his own hands around the dream himself, more or less exploring it as the beginning of a dialogue with what we've all now come to call our "inner child," I waited for a lull in his own associations and reflections before I asked simply, "Again?"

We had worked long enough together, he and I, that I didn't really need to say anything more, and I remember quite distinctly the whole mood of the session between us suddenly shifting in a way that I couldn't, initially, figure out. I could see he had remembered something he had forgotten—something really powerful and moving—and that he was at the same time a little stunned that, given its importance, he had forgotten it. There was a long silence and finally he said, "I hadn't really put that together. But yes, that's what this is about. However, why

I'm dreaming of this now," he looked at me, "I guess that's for you and me to figure out."

"You and I have never talked about this, because until now," he continued, "we've never really had a need to, I suppose, which is a little strange because it's kind of a big thing from my childhood, but I've never even talked to my own parents about it, mostly because I could never figure out how, or maybe, why." He shrugged. "But, in short, I guess what I'll say is that, yes, I know the young boy in this photograph in my dream, and it's my childhood imaginary friend Steve. I've never told you about my imaginary friend Steve, have I?"

I smiled. "Uh, no. Children's imaginary friends are usually pretty important to them, so if you had, I'd remember."

"Are they?" Quentin laughed. "Mine was, for sure. And I won't have you tell me about what they mean," he said, a bit wryly, because he knew I would probably deflect a generic question like that and beg off from lecturing in favor of asking him about his imaginary friend in particular, so he just got busy. I had trained him well as a client of mine.

"So, yeah, I had an imaginary friend named Steve when I was little, and I don't know about other kids and their imaginary friends, but my recollection about Steve was he was a part of my early life from about age four or five. Things are a little hazy but I seem to remember coming home from kindergarten or first grade and telling him about what had happened during the day, maybe because I was youngest out of the six of us, and I knew that my older siblings wouldn't be interested. I had a bunch of stuffed animals when I was little—again lots of older siblings, lots of hand-me-down stuffed animals—and when I was in pre-school, I used to tell them all about my thoughts and feelings, but Steve kinda came into my life when I was a little older, and he was, I guess I would say, primarily a conversation partner. He and I didn't go out and do things together. He lived in my room, actually specifically he lived in my clothes closet, and he rarely came out of there. Every once in a while, he might venture out into the room I shared with my two brothers if they weren't there and I had something to show him. Otherwise, what it mostly looked like was me, sitting in front of the closet, having a conversation with Steve while I was drawing, or putting something together, or a little later doing my homework. Sometimes these conversations were out loud, and occasionally people like my mom would catch me and ask me who I was talking to, and I would just say that I was talking to myself, but I'm sure she, at least, figured out that I had an imaginary friend, though I never admitted to it, and I certainly never told her his name or anything about him. And naturally, you can imagine, I got pretty adept at having entirely unspoken conversations with Steve that went on more or less in my head after getting caught and teased by my two older brothers, sitting in front of the closet talking to no one. In fact, a lot of these con-versations went on internally, and I wouldn't say they were especially deep or dramatic or anything. Steve and I just kinda hung out.

"But I will say a couple of things about him. I had a very clear visual image of him, he was my size and my age, but thinner and a little smaller, bright red hair, and always dressed in jeans and a white T-shirt. I drew a couple of pictures of him when I was little, pictures of him and me doing things and going on adventures, maybe because the two of us never left the room. I remember one of them was us climbing a mountain, and another one was the two of us skiing. They were both after Mom and Dad took us up to Tahoe for a winter vacation one year, so I guess you could say that the pictures were my way of taking Steve along with me, after the fact, as it were.

"Now for the longest time, as I got older, I would think about Steve my imaginary friend with whom, I would say, at around maybe age 9 or 10, I ceased having conversations with, grew out of it, and made real friends with whom I would hang out and do things after school; I didn't really need an imaginary friend anymore. And so, at that point, Steve became sort of a childhood memory, you know, a little bit like your favorite stuffed animal that once upon a time seemed alive and real but now you look on with sentimental affection and you remember the conversations you used to have, but you know, it's a stuffed animal." Quentin laughed. "Anyway, the image in this dream looks a lot like Steve looked in my mind's eye, and it's a little weird, because I haven't thought of him in a *long, long* time."

I took in what Quentin was telling me with a lot of thought, but I was noticing during his description of his relationship to this childhood friend that he kept glancing away from me and out of the window in an uncharacteristic way, and I just knew there was more to the story.

"Soooooo......? I said in my best therapist voice.

Quentin cocked an eyebrow. "Soooooo.....let me think a bit when I found out...I'd say I was probably about 15 or 16 at the time and was still at home. In fact, I was the only one of the kids still at home. My older brother and his wife had been expecting a baby, but pretty early on in the pregnancy, she miscarried, which of course was really hard for them and for all of us. I was talking about it with one of my other older brothers who let it drop that my mom had also had a miscarriage. Now that was something I knew absolutely nothing about at the time, no one in the family ever discussed it, and just the way he talked about it himself, very gingerly, I could pick up that it was a very painful subject and therefore a bit of a family secret. So, I asked him about it, and he said as much, you know, sorta, 'don't tell Mom I told you but...' And as it turns out, it was less of a miscarriage but had actually been a very advanced pregnancy between my oldest brother and my next oldest sister. She ended up losing the baby because of some kind of genetic birth defect or something like that. My brother said the baby was 6 or 7 months along, so it was something more like a stillborn birth for my mom, which is why my brother's wife's miscarriage was hitting her so hard at the time.

"So, I'm listening to this story from my brother when I'm about 15, hearing about all this for the first time when he says, 'And John told me that Mom and Dad actually had the pastor christen the baby after it was born, even though it was dead, so that they could bury it in the cemetery with Grandma and Grampa.'

"And I'm listening to him, going, 'like, really?' when he then says, 'They named him Stephen, which is Grampa's middle name, and John told me they did that so that when they went to the grave, Grampa's headstone would be a way to remember baby Stephen without having a whole separate burial plot."

"You can imagine the impact of getting this bit of family information, especially in the midst of my brother having lost his own first baby just then, and frankly at the time, talking to Tom, I really didn't put it together myself, until I went back to my room that night and then it hit me: my imaginary friend Steve was actually my older/baby brother Stephen. Don't ask me how I knew, and Lord knows I had never told anyone about my imaginary friend, Steve—no one knew, absolutely no one, least of all my mom. And since then, I really have no cogent explanation for it, because maybe, just maybe, I had somehow picked up information, you know the way kids do, around the edges, that my mother had had a miscarriage before I was born. The woman had four children after all, and my sister Susie's birth was pretty complicated, she had to stay in bed for months, lots of family stories about that, so I very well may have subconsciously picked up the information about the miscarriage, but there is absolutely no way that I had ever been told that the stillborn child had been named Stephen—I mean, not just named, but actually formally christened by our pastor—and then had been buried with my grandparents. Now that is all specific information there's no way I would have forgotten or repressed."

Quentin paused and look at me. "Soooooo....that's who I am dreaming about here. I haven't thought of Steve in a long, long time, and I think maybe you are the third person I have ever told about how the imaginary friend I had in my childhood was in reality—I don't know what you would call it—the ghost, the spirit, the presence of my older brother who I never knew, who no one ever knew. I really don't know what to make of his appearance, because, as I said, to me, he was red-haired, young, eternally five years old, and if we went by the ages, when I was five or so, he would have been 12 or 13. But I really can't get around the coincidence of his name. That's the detail that feels incredibly synchronistic to me, because there's no way I could have made that up myself. I didn't even know my grandfather, no less his middle name, no less know that my mother had named the child she lost, an older brother I never knew, Stephen.

"But sitting with this dream, I know that periodically I have dreams of him, and really at this point in my life, I guess I would say that I think of him as a kind of guardian angel or spirit, and maybe he was a little like that for me as a child, he came to be with me during a time when I needed a friend. I don't really know. But that's who's in the living photograph of this dream, my imaginary friend, my older/baby brother, Steve."

There's an eeriness, perhaps, about this story which bears mentioning, and it was certainly something I felt while Quentin was telling it to me, and definitely Quentin himself felt not just in the telling but in the living of it. Depth psychologists have taken to use a specific term to describe this feeling that happens when a deep level of the unconscious rises to the surface in an unexpected, unbidden way, which is particularly true about a lot of synchronistic events that happen to us: they are, we would say, uncanny. The psychological use of this term comes directly from Freud and his original essay on the experience, appropriately named "The Uncanny." Being Freud, of course, he adopted this word to describe that particular feeling state which accompanies the breaking through of unconscious contents that are forbidden, taboo, unacceptable or threatening, hence the somewhat negative cast to the term, especially in the original German in which *unheimlich* means literally "un-secret" or "un-concealed."

Since then, we've all come to use that word in a far less technical way, to convey the goose-flesh-inducing quality of any number of things—the plot twists of Gothic novels, the suspenseful tension of Hitchcock movies, the extraordinary accuracy and knowledge of various savants or performers that leaves us marveling at what is being revealed, bit by bit. But I believe there are times when the original and more precisely psychological sense of the term should be resurrected and applied, and I believe Quentin's story is one of those times. Uncanny is an apt term to express not just the emotional feeling of such an event, its spookiness, but, in following Freud's usage, the very nature of a synchronistic event itself. And in a way, the English word "uncanny" goes even farther in this direction than Freud's original German, because it comes not from a sense of concealment or hiddenness but even more straightforwardly from the root word "ken" in old English, which means "to know." Hence, as we say, a canny person is someone who *knows* how to get something done, who knows what's up, who understands the deeper levels of a situation or a person. By contrast, then, an *uncanny* event is eerie to us precisely because it brings up to our awareness what we *know* unconsciously. Quentin's dream became the occasion of entree into a whole realm of unconscious relationship to a brother he had always known and yet, simultaneously, had never known. It was only through the synchronistic events of his life that the full awareness of his lived and unlived relationship to his brother came to the surface.

It's the rich inner significance of these dynamics which, in my opinion, makes any potential causal explanation for Quentin's story fall flat. Sure, one may say that as a small child, before full self-awareness, before language, he had picked up on subliminal communications about his deceased brother, a word here, a glance here, the casual mention of a name, maybe in passing, and had somehow put it all together into the fantasy of his imaginary friend. But again, none of that goes to the emotionally dramatic nature of his later discovery that this friend and his brother were indeed one in the same. That is what makes his experience synchronistic. Indeed, a synchronistic event has its psychological significance precisely because of this intersection of the deep unconscious and our conscious, daytime experience—and *that* is always an uncanny experience for us—uncanny in every sense.

Christopher Bollas, the British psychoanalyst, has come to be identified with a very similar concept which became the title of his best-known book, *The Shadow of the Object: Psychoanalysis of the Unthought Known.* Drawn from a comment Freud made originally to a patient in which he suggested to a patient that an experience he had uncovered in the course of his treatment was something the patient had always *known* but had never *thought,* Bollas's work goes on to explore the way in which our very early experiences in childhood that predate our ability to speak or understand language—our preverbal experiences— have fundamental importance in shaping our sense of self, our sense of others, and our expectations of the world and how it works—or at least how we think it *should* work. As a Freudian, of course, Bollas coined this expression of the "unthought known" primarily with reference to what Jungians on the other side of the theoretical divide would come to call more specifically our personal unconscious—that is to say, all those elements of our experience which we have lived in our lives but which at any given moment in time aren't present in our awareness, either due to memory or repression. However, for Jung, the idea of the "unthought known" of our experience could be even further expanded to include those elements of our common human experience which he came to call archetypal, those basic experiences of our inner lives which we share with all other persons on the planet as a collective unconscious.

Quentin's synchronistic experience, in all its uncanniness, is a near classic example of an unthought known, touching as it does upon not simply his own personal unconscious experience, his own preverbal knowing, but bringing forward on the archetypal level the way in which our experience of relatedness is fundamental to our humanity. Though he was not privy to specific facts that would have allowed him to *think about* his brother, he nevertheless *knew* he had one, and only much later in life, having lived with the unthought known of this relationship in his interior life throughout his childhood, and even for many years until his adulthood, his discovery of the external truth of it was a synchronistic event that brought together both the personal unconscious with the archetypal experience of his familial, sibling bond that had theretofore only been able to be expressed in the form of an "imaginary" friend. This synchronistic event, we might say, confirmed that he had always known but what he had not been able to think, and that what he knew—what we all know—is that relationship, our family relationships, and particularly our relationships to our brothers and sisters, our first peers and companions in life, is fundamental to our sense of self in the world.

Finally, a story from a long-time acquaintance of mine named David is a good illustration of a similar dynamic unconsciously ensconced in a pair of synchronistic events wherein his sister *knew* something she couldn't have and what she knew brought them together as siblings synchronistically.

"My relationship to my family," David began, "had never been good or easy. My two sisters and my parents, I felt, were always much more in tune with one another then I was. My father had, like many fathers, largely gone at work, my mother and two sisters had a bond with one another as girls and women that as a boy, I felt outside of. I never quite fit in well with the general extraversion of the family's overall style—they loved parties, activities, going out, doing things, while I was always a fairly introverted child—preferred my room, reading, quiet activities, socially awkward, especially when being forced to interact or dragged along to picnics or church events. Then, slowly, as I became aware at an early age of my homosexuality, I had the experience I think many gay boys have of being apart from the others, different. Put that together with my natural shyness, and I would say that, more or less by my teenage years, my sisters along with my parents had kind of given up on making a connection with me. I have described myself as having been an only child in a family of five, and even in the pictures you see it. They are all a big clump, looking in the same direction, smiling, and there's David, me, looking away or looking vacant or slightly turned or strangely dressed.

"I was lucky to have a couple of teachers who 'got' me in high school, one of whom was obviously if not publicly gay, and thanks to their support, I managed to do pretty well in school, again not a value my parents were especially enthusiastic about, my father would have clearly much preferred a popular star athlete to go with my two bouncy popular cheerleader sisters, but of course they didn't complain about my academic achievements. However, I knew I was going to be getting the heck out of Dodge as soon as possible by going away to school, and the only place I applied were across the country, which is how I ended up in California.

"The estrangement between us started then, and once it got put into place geographically it never really shifted. I think my parents came out to visit me maybe twice, and neither of my sisters ever did. Each of them were way too busy with their own lives, boyfriends, friends, school, vacations, and the pair of them stayed pretty close to my hometown, went to school in state, and one of them dated and eventually married her high school boyfriend. It was around about college graduation time when I finally came out to them, and really only did that because my whole senior year I had had a boyfriend and the two of us were planning to move in together for grad school, at which point I figured I might as well tell them all who this Harry was that I would be living with over on Cedar Street and that it wasn't just an air-quote roommate. Even that wasn't, I would say, a big deal, I remember doing it on the phone one night with my parents who by then I'm pretty sure had figured it out, and the fact is that I never actually formally came out to my sisters. There was never a time when I sat down with them or wrote them or called them and said, 'Gail, Rhonda, I'm gay.' That's really the level of non-interaction we had by that point.

"I call it estrangement, but understand by that, I don't mean it was tense or hostile. We just simply didn't relate to one another. We were brother and sister but we didn't have a relationship, and really never had. I ascribed it to their self-centeredness—they had full lives and always had and really never seemed to want to be bothered with curiosity about me or my life—so they just sailed along, and I didn't really have any need to connect myself to them, which would have taken a lot of effort, and besides, we didn't have much in common.

"So, there we are in our late 20s, but then Harry and I are graduated, I'm teaching, he's running his restaurant, things are good, and I get word from my sister Gail that she and Rhonda are coming out to the Bay Area for a girls-only vacation, the two of them and I think a couple of their other girlfriends, you know, their posse, as we say these days—husbands are staying home, just the girls. As I'm talking to Gail, though, which is really maybe the first time in years, I would say, I'm feeling like we're kind of having the first adult-adult conversation ever, which I'll admit was pretty nice. She's actually asking me questions about my life, about Harry, about my teaching job, and I'm hearing behind the scenes, I'd say, a little bit of remorse about the distance between us. And clearly, she and Rhonda probably could have come out to San Francisco for a trip with their girlfriends and not even let me know, but here she was making a point of it.

"Anyway, Harry, of course, has never met any of my family and he suggests that we have them over for dinner to our then itsy-bitsy little Berkeley northside apartment where we were living at the time. I'm, like, sure, why not, he's a great cook, my sisters will love him, because he's the host with the most at the restaurant, so I run it by Gail and she's thrilled. Sure, she and Rhonda would love to make time for dinner at our place.

"They get here to San Francisco, and I'm getting the basic updates via text. At this point, we're not conversing on the phone, just exchanging texts about what they are doing, Golden Gate Bridge, Muir Woods, you know, all the tourist things. As far as I know, we're on for dinner, so the day comes and Harry's doing Harry's typical thing, full-on four courses, elaborate by anyone else's standards, naturally, but he's got set ideas about how dinner needs to go—appetizers, salad, main, and dessert, all local, all fresh. On Cedar Street, the kitchen was not big, and there really was room for just the four of us, but as the evening approaches, I find myself getting frankly kind of excited. Underneath it, I would say that I was feeling, maybe hoping, maybe wanting, the evening to be a turning point for us as siblings. I liked that they were coming to my place, to our space, that me and my boyfriend were showing them our lives, how we lived, what we enjoyed, and just the tenor of the conversations and texts between me and them by that point all suggested that the three of us were ready to turn the corner.

"So, as I said, we don't have a big place back then, it's our old grad school apartment under rent control, and we just didn't want to disrupt our lives or our budget to move. But the way Harry likes to entertain, it's a bit of a hassle, and the day of the dinner, he decides that we are going to make it a special occasion and we are going to have Schramsberg champagne from Napa Valley with his dessert, which I think was something like meringues or I don't know. But the champagne, absolutely. However, huge crisis—he and I do not have champagne flutes, and I guess that's a big deal. We can't possibly use our regular wine glasses, we have to get flutes.

"I remember pushing back a little on the issue—where are we going to put a set of champagne flutes, not to mention, champagne flutes that in all likelihood we're going to use once for his dinner, to put on the dog for my two sisters, no less, whom I haven't seen for years.

So, I'm saying basically, forget about it, and he's in a dither, wants to make a good impression. We almost get into a fight about it, because he wants me to run around town trying to find them that afternoon, and I'm more or less saying to him, get a grip, I'm not running around Berkeley looking for champagne flutes, and there's all the regular couples, 'I'm cooking dinner, couldn't you just help' and I'm saying 'you're the one who decided to go full-on Martha Stewart, not me, and really I don't even know if my clueless sisters will give a shit.' So I do *not* go out for champagne flutes, much to Harry's consternation and that's that.

"The doorbell rings about 6, and there they are, Gail and Rhonda, in all their glory, and it was just very striking how in that one moment so much of our previous 20 years of non-relatedness in a way simply evaporated. It was clear that they had grown up. It was clear I had grown up. It was clear that our personality differences that had been so stark throughout our childhood seemed strangely and quite suddenly irrelevant. They had softened, I would say, no longer self-centered teenage girls but full-grown adult women, and of course I had changed entirely from the weird little shy introvert to a grown-up myself, with a life and a relationship, welcoming them into my home, my boyfriend making them a wonderful dinner.

"Within the first fifteen minutes, therefore, I would say, it was as if the whole previous history of ours had faded into the past, so much so that I remember it feeling a little bit surreal, seeing Gail and Rhonda, in my living room, around my table, talking food and wine with Harry, talking career and apartments with me. Surreal and, to tell the truth, really, really wonderful, like a whole piece of who I was suddenly had clicked into place. There was the sense that these two really *knew* me, knew me since when I was little, knew me in a way none of my California friends, or even my boyfriend, knew me or could know me.

"Dinner was amazing, of course, Harry cooked to impress, and it was also amazing how the time flew by, suddenly it's getting late, and

I say something like, 'I hope you have room, because Harry has made a great dessert,' and he goes to start telling them the story about the Schramsberg and champagne flutes when Rhonda stands up and says, 'Damn, girl,' to Gail, 'Where'd you leave it?' and Gail says, 'Oh that's right! Hang on, boys, we brought you something but left it in the car.' So, she takes off and comes back with a big bag from Sur La Table in which there is—no kidding—a bottle of chilled Schramsberg and a box of four champagne flutes.

"The two of us just screamed and started laughing, because it was ridiculous, I mean, how could they have possibly known, first, that we ourselves had a bottle of Schramsberg in the refrigerator and, two, that we had practically spent the whole afternoon fighting about goddamn champagne flutes. So, Harry whips out his own bottle of Schramsberg to show them, and Rhonda says, 'We know ZERO about California wine, but the guy in the liquor store suggested this was a good one, and we were shopping today and definitely wanted to bring you two something and we figured why not?'"

"Seriously. An unbelievable coincidence. I still think back on it, and as a matter of fact, I still have those champagne flutes in a box in the back of my front hall closet. So sure, it was an amazing coincidence but not just because of how crazy it is the two of them picked that wine and that gift for us but because really of what it meant, in a way, to me. That they *got* me. They were meeting *me* in *my* life. Is it too much to say that they were *attuned* to me? That's how it felt. And it was the way in which I think, if you want to say it this way, that I believe and maybe always unconsciously had always believed that brothers and sisters should feel about one another. It's just that the three of us hadn't. But that crazy coincidence that night, our first night together as grown-ups, in which they brought us our favorite champagne which we then poured into the four glasses, which we needed and didn't have, but which they bought us and brought to us, let us toast that night to family, and we really meant it."

There are quite a few elements of David's story which of course tug at the heartstrings in ways that led me to choose the title of this book, because the very nature of coincidences, indeed, the literal meaning of the actual word, has to do with things, people, events coming together. In fact, one of the phrases I often use when speaking about synchronicity in general but certainly family-related synchronistic events is that they are often like a "great coming together" of people, places and things, inside and outside, past, present and future. Here, with David and his sisters, we have not the sort of synchronistic event that comes out of nowhere dramatically and shockingly but rather the beautifully unexpected culmination of a very intentional rapprochement between these previously estranged siblings. That's where, as I have said through-out, I find myself not especially dumbfounded when a meaningful coincidence occurs in the midst of a life transition, and in some ways, I have come, in my own life and in the life of clients, friends and family, almost to expect such a "coming together."

It's been frequently said that these synchronistic events read almost like short stories or novels, the sort of thing that one almost expects in fiction, so it does become a bit uncanny when they actually happen to us in "real" life. And the skeptics among my readers or in the audience often argue that, indeed, the significance of such events is "made up" by the participants. The events occur as they do, and in retrospect those to whom they have occurred do indeed "make" a meaning out it, fashion a "story" that, for all intents and purposes, is like the creation of a narrative. As I think is clear by now, however, the story is not just invented out of whole cloth and pure imagination, but in a way, the skeptics are not incorrect: it is still a narrative, an interior narrative based on the actual events of one's life which, frankly like all our lives, are sometimes entirely random, unexpected and even at times unwanted but which by virtue of the story we tell, made meaningful, made coherent, made psychologically and interpersonally satisfying the way a great work of fiction is.

Jung often contended that the purpose of his analytic work was not to "cure illness," because he tended not to think in such starkly medical terms of psychopathology, but since after all people do come to psychotherapy in pain and suffering to find a way forward and out to happiness and fulfillment, he felt that the closest thing he might concede to be a cure in psychotherapy would be creative expression. In other words, if a patient could find his or her way to creatively, imaginatively, and comprehensively *express* themselves, then the meaning created out of that expression would have the result of achieving a certain stability and resolution for the patient that would allow them to rejoice in the good and hold the bad that had occurred to them in a single, coherent, and therefore satisfying, fashion.

That's where I found the specific symbols of David's synchronistic reunion with his sister—the glasses and the champagne—so apt. The fundamental function of glasses is, in the end, to contain and with his sisters' arrival at his apartment, a "full set" of these beautiful, delicate and yet solid and functional containers arrived—a very fitting symbol for what was happening emotionally and interpersonally. Each different, each holding its own contents—there were after all four separate glasses—and yet all four belonging together as a set, a stable and coherent unit, meant to be together as one.

The containment symbolism here cannot help but remind me of one of Jung's more famous discussions concerning synchronicity, from his introduction to the German translation of the I Ching by his friend Richard Wilhelm. Initially that Jung would write an introduction to such a work of ancient Chinese philosophical spirituality, not being, as he himself put it, a "Sinologue," may seem quite out of place, but it was not purely due to his acquaintance with Wilhelm the translator. This venerable work of Chinese culture which dates back nearly two millennia arguably might be characterized as a kind of Bible—one of the classic written works of Chinese culture that forms the basis of a certain way of seeing the world. In the case of the I Ching, the text consists of 64 separate sections or chapters, each of which is devoted to describing what I might best call a "perceptible state of energy," and so the whole volume taken as a whole with all the subsequent commentary is intended to provide a comprehensive description of the entire, eternal flow of life energy through the world and through us. Thus, it is often called in English "the Book of Changes," for that is indeed the very purpose of it: to describe the ever-changing nature of reality by focusing, one by one, on 64 discrete points in the cycle of life, charting with great subtlety and insight how and when life energy flows or does not, how and when life energy stabilizes or becomes unstable, when energies are in harmony or when they are in conflict, using in general quite evocative symbols drawn from both the natural world and human culture.

However, I might venture to say quite *unlike* the Bible of Western culture, the I Ching, this Book of Changes, was not ever meant simply to state the truth of cosmological reality once and for all—this is one place where East does *not* meet West. Instead, the supremely practical nature of Chinese culture can be seen by the way in which the I Ching was meant from the beginning to be used quite practically, directly and consciously applied, day to day in the lives of the Chinese people, and they did so through use of divination. Curious as to what might be the state of energy beneath or below the surface of your daily events? Beginning in ancient times, the Chinese would throw coins and draw straws, look at the patterns created by this random action, and correlate these patterns to one of the specific chapters of the I Ching, thereby divining, through random chance, what place in the cycle of life, what moment of the 64 specific moments, characterized this one, right here and right now.

Given his own concept of synchronicity, therefore, we should not be surprised that Jung found this venerable work of special interest, insofar as it had been used for thousands of years as a modality of spiritual and psychological insight through divination. The very principle of divination of all sorts is essentially identical to Jung's own thoughts about synchronicity, both of which are based on the idea that a random chance pattern in nature—the throw of the coins for the I Ching, the pattern of the tea leaves or the Tarot cards or the vibrations of the dowsing stick—indicate and reveal the underlying state of things below our conscious awareness.

So, in keeping with the divinatory nature of the I Ching itself, Jung felt it entirely appropriate that, instead of simply sitting down and writing your basic scholarly, psychological introduction for the first German edition of it ever published, he should actually use the book itself and ask the I Ching itself what his introduction to it should be. So, Jung threw coins six times, as prescribed by one traditional Chinese method of obtaining an indication for a specific chapter, came up with the chapter entitled "the Cauldron," number 50, the text of which, Jung felt, in its own somewhat symbolic and indirect way indicated that the Book of Changes itself was like a cauldron—a large, voluminous container which had been created specifically to hold together a lot of material in a single place and to do so, stably, for a sufficiently long period of time such that the contents in the cauldron ultimately would be transformed, if not by magic—as in the stereotypical image of a witch's cauldron, say from Macbeth, bubble, bubble, toil and trouble, eye of newt, toe of frog—then less mystically, by simple time and patience, spiritually and psychologically. Thus, what Jung made of his synchronicity experiment was that the I Ching was telling him that it was the Cauldron, the big container of wisdom of all Chinese culture, and moreover, that it "told" him that synchronistically, that is, *through* the random chance pattern made by the coins Jung had thrown to obtain that result.

Now, as a striking and as delightful as the coincidence of David's champagne flutes ended up being for him, his partner and his sisters in its emotional impact—their lovely reunion gift being utterly, unintentionally the very thing that he and his partner had spent the afternoon fussed about—once again I think an equally important element, as with all synchronistic events, is its symbolism. Like the cauldron of the I Ching, David is given a literal set of containers, that is literal physical containers, glasses, that will be holding literal physical champagne, but these stand for a set of containers in a much more symbolic and emotional sense: his sisters and his partner coming together in an important way for the first time as adult *as a family*.

Is it not our families who hold us together, who contain, who transform, each different, as were these individual flutes, and yet each belonging to a single set, each retaining what's inside and yet also displaying, showing through the transparency of the glass what is both inside and out? That's the wonder of a symbol, that it can be not only what it is literally but that it can also stand for, and represent, essential aspects of our being, in this case, aspects of what it means to be family, and that that, too, is what it means to be "family." All these stories of sibling synchronicities, though different, show the unifying thread of connection that bring us together as family, like it or not, conscious or not, a single container that holds within its breadth and depth a multiplicity of individuals, bonds and meanings for each of us.

CHAPTER FOUR

The Past is Not Past: Synchronicity and Our Family History

My friend Jackie is a rather matter-of-fact sort of person, and so not especially someone I might have expected to come forward with a story of synchronicity when she heard about my writing this book. We were at a friend's birthday party when the topic came up and she was immediately curious, in line with what I would say is her generally thoughtful, if not intellectual/science-nerdy/research-oriented approach to all things that I put down to both her temperament as well as her training as a physician. "Meaningful coincidences?" she joked a bit with me, "as opposed, say, to meaningless coincidences?"

"Exactly," I joked back. "Sometimes a cigar is just a cigar, but the synchronistic events that I'm writing about are coincidences that people have found important to them in the course of their life, and this book in particular is going to be coincidences between family members."

"Well," she said, "I definitely have one of those, and in a way, I guess you could say, it's why I'm a doctor."

I raised my eyebrows that evening and pointed right at her. "We'll talk."

Which is what we did the following week over lunch, my treat.

"So," Jackie began, "the latter part of the story doesn't make a whole lot of sense unless you understand the first part of the story, which really has to do with the family I grew up in. Lovely family, on the whole, maybe more than most, I would say, and certainly, I'm sure, more than what comes into your office. I was loved, I was cared for, both my brothers and me, and my parents are very middle-of-the-road, normal stable people, but it's a family of teachers.

"Both my father and mother had been teachers their whole lives, my father taught English at the high school level for years and years and years at a school in nearby town, my mother started as an elementary school teacher and gradually worked her way through the school system to actually become principal at the elementary school where my brothers and I had gone in our hometown. My two older brothers likewise, following in the family tradition, went to college and aimed for careers in teaching as well, which they have eventually succeeded in. The one teaches in the English department at a private university near our hometown, specializes in medieval literature, the other is almost like a clone of my dad, and he teaches English at a local high school where he and his wife ended up settling down. And the teaching profession is a long family tradition which didn't just start with my parents. My grandfather, my father's father, had been an academic, too, in his time, somewhat of a name at the state university where my dad went, served as chairman of the department there, and his wife, my grandmother, wasn't an academic herself but kept herself very involved as a volunteer/teacher's aide in the educational system all throughout her life, not to mention her unacknowledged lifetime role as 'faculty wife' to the department chair. I do think that in a different time and place, she herself would have gone to college, gotten a degree and perhaps joined the faculty, but that was then and this is now.

"So, with my family, I grew up more or less surrounded by teachers and teaching, to which I would definitely attribute my own love for learning, intellectual curiosity, my discipline around reading and writing. However, as I just said, all of their areas of study and professional work were definitely the liberal arts, English, philosophy, art history in the case of my mother, and none of them were especially gifted, I would say, in the areas of science, mathematics, engineering, technology, you know, the hard sciences. Except me. Something about science for me from an early age just 'fit,' I don't know how to describe it. The factual quality of it, the definite black and white aspect of it—something is either true or it isn't, period—and yet, there's the creative aspect of generating theories and then hypotheses, testing them in the real world, gathering data, confirming, disconfirming, revising, re-testing—all of it was and has always been frankly kind of thrilling to me. As soon as I took my very first biology course in junior high, I knew somewhere deep down, this was the field where I belonged.

"Looking back now, I really can't say why I felt it necessary to keep all of my interest in science so much of a secret. I was an excellent student in all my classes, so I just let my parents conclude that my good biology and chemistry grades were because I was their smart kid, but I do know that my excellence in English and the arts were evidence to them that I would be following in everyone's footsteps. So that might have been a part of it, I would have had to buck the trend. And back then, I do think being a girl played into some of this as well, because there was a general sense around town that the smartest kids would all become doctors of some sort—medical doctors or dentists, or do their doctorates in areas like physics or engineering—but of course all the doctors I ever knew were men. Girls went into nursing. Men became doctors. So, if you aren't presented with the possibility, you don't ever see any women in jobs like that, and you're not actually encouraged to consider it as a profession, it simply doesn't occur to you.

"But, by the time I was in college, going forward to become a physician did occur to me, because somewhat passively, I ended up going to the liberal arts college where both my brothers and my father had gone, and by the end of my freshmen year, I was not a happy camper. I felt stuck instead in an English literature program that really wasn't grabbing me, and I found myself really missing the top-notch science classes I had had in my high school. So, by that summer after my first year, following lots of conversations on campus with friends and some really helpful faculty and academic advisors—I think I even saw a counselor on campus a couple of times—I knew I was going to need to have a talk with my parents to tell them I wanted to transfer to the big state university nearby and enroll in their pre-med program.

"I didn't have any idea how my parents would take it, because since it all might now mean an extra year of schooling to make up pre-reqs that I had missed this first year around, and back then, unlike now, people did not take five years to finish a four-year college unless something was very wrong. And plus, you know, I came from a family of teachers. At the time, it did feel like a potential explosive revelation of who I really was to them, perhaps for the first the time in my life. Now, I was a 19-year old girl at the time and of course everything feels big and dramatic at that age, but this aspect of me, a girl, going against a long family tradition, let's say, it loomed large.

"So, I go home that summer, fired up for whatever may happen, once I tell them that I'm going to be leaving Dad's alma mater and want instead to go to medical school and become a doctor, and not just a doctor, but, I had decided, a doctor with a specialty in epidemiology and infectious diseases. Somehow that had captured my imagination, because in the age of HIV almost 30 years ago, it was all very much in the news, and the doctors and scientists back then really seemed to me to be rather heroic figures, engaged in an important mission, saving lives, changing the world. Again, I'm not ashamed to admit, a 19-year-old teenage girl's version of finding her vocation in medicine, but that's how it was."

Jackie laughed. "In the end, the conversation with my wonderful parents was a total non-event. On the contrary, they felt a little bad that they hadn't really picked up on my unhappiness at school that year, and neither one of them had any issue whatsoever with my intention to go into a pre-med program at the university. And as a matter of fact, with their own academic connections, they were able to get me situated that summer in a pair of intensive courses which would serve to move me along the way to making up for the pre-requisites I could have and should have been taking that first, wasted, year. And in any case, due to scheduling, I wasn't even going to be able to apply to transfer until the next year, which in itself wasn't too terrible, because I did have plenty to make-up. So, in the interim, I was able to get a decent job and put away some money, but psychologically, emotionally, it was a tough 'break year' for me. Remember this was a time when kids didn't do that sort of thing, and, despite my parents' support, I, of course, am now having the real experience in doing my pre-med coursework, one of maybe only two or three women in classes full of guys, so at that point I'm now really getting a taste of what it's going to mean to be a woman in a man's field, not to mention, ultimately, an epidemiological researcher. It was tough.

"So that's when the synchronistic event occurred. My dear mother one day shows up in my room with an old shoebox full of letters, and she says to me, 'I really don't know why I haven't thought of this, but did you know that your great-uncle was a doctor?' I did not. Which is when she tells me his story for the first time. So, my great-grand-uncle, my mother's grandmother's brother, was, as it turns out, not just an obstetrician, but the only obstetrician in the little town where my mother grew up, and God bless him, he went to med school at Columbia just after the turn of the century. And the whole time he was there, he wrote these letters to my mother's aunt, my great-aunt, about his time in New York. I remember my mother laughing and saying, 'You know what a packrat Grandma was, she held onto everything, and when I was downstairs yesterday, looking for something, I saw this box where all the rest of the stuff from her house is down there, and looking through them, I realized that these are the letters Oscar wrote to Lena in med school. Given everything, I thought you might find them interesting. I have no idea what's in them, but I do know he was at Columbia Med School at the time, and who knows what's in them....'

"I confess, I was more than a little stunned. I guess, when I think about it, I must have known in a vague way that he had been a doctor but not really. My grandparents, in fact, that whole generation, was long gone by the time I was born, so it wasn't like I knew my grandparents or their brothers or sisters, and we weren't that close to our cousins on that side of the family anyway. But here I was now, preparing to launch myself off into a big fat unknown medical career, and sitting there on my childhood bed with a box of letters from my great-uncle, the doctor, from when he was in med school.

"It was a very cool coincidence, very well-timed, you might say, and quite a find. And beyond the super historical aspect of it all, it was simply fascinating *for me* on so many levels to read his letters. They gave me a little bit of a glimpse of what I would be experiencing before long, the intensity of the training, the full-fledged immersion into a profession which, as I tell interns and residents, is not something you *do* but something instead you *become*, 'doctor' becomes your life and your identity. Just the way he wrote about what he was doing, using his correspondence as a kind of diary, a way of recording what was happening. I found as I read them that I could also identify so much with him in terms of how he thought—so logical and rational, very reflective, a little dry and unemotional, clinical. And there was, as it turns out, one female faculty member at the med school class, a gynecologist, at the time which he mentioned now and then in his letters to his fiancée back home, my eventual great-aunt, at first mentioning her as a bit of a curiosity but then coming to like her and respect her for her seriousness and her intellect. I was curious about her myself, after reading his letter and did a bit of research and found out that she had indeed quite a distinguished career, so that was quite inspiring to my teenage self.

"Anyway, this cache of letters my mother had forgotten about landed in my lap that summer just when I needed it to, and that's the synchronistic aspect of it, yes? Not because the coincidence was amazing, and really not because it changed anything externally, but it was very important to me on so many levels because, until then, I had felt quite alone in my family, going off in a direction none of them had gone before. But then, I discovered that was not true, and that medicine as a profession was in fact a part of my larger family's tradition and heritage. Also, what had an impact on me was what he had written about his woman professor and some of his female classmates. Here I was, feeling quite isolated as a young woman setting off to join a very male-dominated profession, and through my great-uncle's correspondence, I read about woman colleagues of his who had done the same for themselves and had made a successful go of it.

"It's hard to describe the effect of those couple dozen letters from a member of my family I had never even met, but they grounded me. They confirmed me in my path. They gave me the sense that I belonged, that who I was and what I was going to be doing had a place, and that it was a genuine vocation for our larger family, if not for my immediate family. I still have those letters, and I keep them in my office on the bookshelf. At some point, I'll probably donate them to Columbia. My great-uncle really helped me, and if I was more of a religious or spiritual person, I might say he was my patron saint or guardian angel as a doctor."

In his play *Requiem for a Nun*, the great Southern writer William Faulkner gave us a line that is often quoted because of its universal truth. "The past is never dead; it isn't even past." Jackie's story, indeed all the stories in this chapter, are demonstrations of Faulkner's insight about the relationship between past and present, and perhaps nowhere more than in our family experience does the living past get brought to our attention. Who among us hasn't sat down with our relatives and in looking through the photo album noted how the shape of a smile or the posture of a long gone relative bears such a striking resemblance to someone in our current family with whom we share our lives, our mother, our son...? Who doesn't cherish a piece of jewelry, a handmade blanket, a piece of art that once belonged to Mother or Auntie or Grandmama? Indeed, the past is never dead, it isn't even past—in our families, we experience the ongoing reality of our history daily and these resemblances or treasures are the sort of connections we have almost come to expect. Practically inherent in the very concept of family is the word that Jackie herself used to describe one part of her experience: tradition. Our families are how our identity—who we are— is handed down to us from generation and generation, and so normal and natural does this relationship between past and present feel that, I would daresay, most of us live our lives rather unconscious of the traditions that surround us and shape us.

That is, until something like a synchronistic event wakes us up. And in Jackie's case, I think it's good to notice exactly what the conditions actually were for that awakening. As the identified "expert on synchronicity," I'm often approached by people, usually after a workshop, class or lecture about synchronicity who want my advice on how they can invite a greater profusion of synchronistic events into their lives. "I read these stories and talk to some people and these things happen to them a lot, but they never happen to me. How can I make them more a part of my path in life?" I try most of the time to be cordial about this request, but frankly, it gets a bit awkward, since meaningful coincidences are not something one can "cause," and so, it's a delicate matter sometimes for me to find a diplomatic way to say that the person asking seems to have pretty much missed the entire point of the concept and perhaps of my entire presentation. These are coincidences, not intentional events; one does not make them happen.

But there are a couple of ways that I have found to respond to this earnest interest in living a fuller and more meaningful life, which is ultimately what I think folks are actually asking my advice on, and both of these are illustrated by a story such as Jackie's. The first I have pointed out a few times already; these events generally occur in times of transition for individuals. Once again, the transitional timing of a synchronistic event was indeed the case when Jackie's mom so thought-fully came across this cache of her great-uncle's medical school letters. Jackie was, in fact, making a number of different life transitions, too, when we think about it. She was moving from one field of study and profession to another, moving from being a child in her family to finding her way in the world, and establishing herself as full-fledged independent adult—individuating, as we psychotherapists put it. She was also navigating her way through a more inward shift in thinking, from a more narrow way of thinking about herself as a woman into a wider way of thinking about who she as a woman might be, could be, or even should be in the world, taking on the task of entering into a field dominated by men and thereby changing it, for herself and for the profession.

So that's my first response to those seeking after synchronicities: look for them in times of transition in your life. Which is to say, I believe it's rather unlikely that something of a synchronistic nature will happen if you go about living your life with the paramount aim of controlling every detail and assuring maximum stability and con-sistency. For as we can see not just in Jackie's story but in many of the stories we have heard so far and certainly in the stories yet to come in this chapter and the next, what we might blithely call a time of transition may be experienced at the time as a great trial, a major and very painful disruption of our life, and perhaps even as misfortune or, worse, a tragedy.

Which brings me to the second thing I say, therefore, to the syn-chronicity seekers: be careful what you wish for because synchronistic events often tend to occur at a point when we are pulling away from one way of being and have not yet found our way forward to the next. To call these phases "liminal," as I have, doesn't get fully to how challenging it can feel to us at the time, and for that reason, I'm very grateful to Jackie for her story, because she was able to communicate quite vividly the stress that she was experiencing in her transition—the fears of what her parents would say, the possibility of losing their respect and support, the palpable difficulties she began to encounter as a minority female within a male majority of her classes.

I have spoken of the family as a container in the last chapter, using the image from the I Ching that was given to Jung, and so it is. Our families do contain, hold, support, nurture. But as we individuate into adulthood and move out of our past and into our own present, fully and intentionally, the container of our family can sometimes feel less like a foundation of support and more like an anchor, dragging us backward and away from the future before us, or even worse sometimes, we may feel the family and its traditions as a prison, barring us altogether from being who we need to be. For all the security our families provide us, there is likewise a shadow side to where we come from, and Jackie's story about setting out upon her own individual destiny certainly illuminates exactly that double-sided quality of "the family tradition," stable but confining, rooted but stultifying. One might well expect, therefore, for unplanned and serendipitous synchronistic events to play an active part in unlocking the process and freeing us up, as they did for Jackie, just at the time when one begins to walk that line between past and present, pushing away from what was in order to step into what will be. That tension was definitely at the forefront of her experience, and even many years later, when she spoke to me as a well-established physician in her own right: the vivid quality of how it felt for her to be that 19-year-old girl comes through.

And so does the wonder of discovering her great-uncle's letters, the way in which, like Jan my musician client, a figure from her family's larger history reaches out across the decades and nearly a century later communicates to her, which throws yet another light on Faulkner's insight. "The past is never dead, it isn't even past" doesn't simply mean we can never escape our history nor is it merely an observation of how all our present moments are interpenetrated by what we lived up to that point. I would say he captured a particular truth about the nature of our families—how our family is the juncture between past and present for each of us, so that never dies nor is ever past is what Jackie discovered quite pointedly in this intimate acquaintance with her uncle, namely, how much we share and will always share with our families. That is certainly what is delightful when we leaf through the photo album and celebrate the resemblances, but it is also what such synchronistic connections likewise bring to our attention: our past, the family's history, comes forward with us and in us as we move forward into our own life fully.

My friend Eddie from my men's group pulled me aside at one of our get-togethers and said to me, "I heard you were doing another book on synchronicity around family relationships and I do have a story of my own that really hit me at the time." So, we grabbed another cup of coffee and went over to the side.

"Now, I think I should preface this a little, because this is a story about my father, and well..." he paused and looked away with a slight smile that I could see hid a fair bit of emotion, "Let's just say that I wouldn't consider my father much of a father. Life with him was very difficult as I was growing up, for me and for my two sisters; he was always very physical with us, and really, it isn't an exaggeration for me to say that he did in many ways make my growing up a nightmare. Eventually, in keeping with what I would say was his generally poor character, he abandoned my mother for another woman, moved back to his mother's property and promptly placed that property in his new wife's name to keep from having to use it to cover child support. I had two sisters under 18 when he left us, and in the end, he never paid a penny. In short, my father was not a good guy.

"Not just because of him, you understand, but because in so many ways where I grew up was just not a place for me to be, I took it upon myself, as soon as I could, to establish myself elsewhere and get my education, and you know, I really never looked back. Now, it was the spring of 1996, and I was driving from a work-related conference in

Washington, D.C. to visit my mother and sisters in Ohio, and along the way, I planned to stop in Lewisburg, West Virginia, and visit with my cousin Arlene and her partner Allen for one night and then head on to Ohio the next day.

"At that point, as you can probably imagine, I really had no reason to go back to West Virginia very often my mother and sisters weren't there. And yet, that's where the family is all from and back then, I still had a lot of family there, among whom were my cousin and her family. So, they and I ended up having a nice overnight visit in Lewisburg, and I took off early the next morning. On my way out of state, really, by complete unplanned chance, I decided to stop in the very tiny community of Sandstone along the New River, about 40 miles from Lewisburg. Sandstone is the nearest town to the little "holler" where my parents grew up—you know how they call those small little communities up in the hills in Appalachia 'hollers.' My parents' holler was referred to as Ramp, and it was about ten miles up past this tiny town of Sandstone.

"Now, I had been to both Ramp and Sandstone plenty when I was a child. Back when our family was whole and we would visit my grandparents, we would often stop in Sandstone on our way back to Ohio and buy some penny candy, or, in my case, a box of Cracker Jacks, in the general store right there. This store, with its gas pumps outside, closely resembled a run-down version of Mr. Drucker's store in *Green Acres*, complete with wooden porch and rocking chairs. Very, very typical small-town store. So, I really don't know what made me do it on this day—I hadn't been there for years and years—but I got the idea of stopping by and picking up a copy of the local newspaper for my mother, some of my older sister's favorite candies—maple nut goodies—as well as a box of Cracker Jacks for me.

"So, I get my stuff, and as I walked up to the counter with my purchases, I see two old men behind the counter playing checkers, and just as the young lady at the register rang up my purchase, one of these old men groused loud enough for me to hear, 'You are such a bull shitter, Harless Hosey!'

"Now, there are very few Hoseys in the world and even fewer Harless Hoseys. And here I was in Sandstone at this store in the middle of nowhere, West Virginia, for the first time in many, many years. So, I looked again and sure enough, recognized that the second fellow playing checkers there was, in fact, my father. He looked much older, as I am sure did I by then with my beard and my own short-cropped, thinning hair all these years later, and I remember he even looked over once, but even though he saw me, he seemed to not have a glimmer of recognition.

"It was a memorable moment. As I handed the cashier the money for my purchases, time seemed to slow to a crawl, and of course, my mind was literally flying through several thoughts and emotions. The first was, should I say anything? I hadn't seen the man in years, many years, and here he was now right in front of me. Was I meant to see him? But then, the second thought, the more important one to me really was, did I *want* to say anything? Given who he was as a father, I had spent most of my younger life being afraid of this man and a good part of the past 15 years since then being angry at him.

"So, standing there at the counter of the general store in front of my father, who I just happened upon due to a spontaneous stop along my way out of state, it took me no more than a few moments to conclude that, insofar as I had not thought of him, either in anger or in fear for such a long while, that no, I had no need for contact. And with that realization, I felt a deep calm come over me. I collected my change and walked out of the store.

"Unfortunately, cell phone service back then was very spotty in the mountains of West Virginia, but given what had just happened, I stopped on the porch of the general store and used the pay phone there to call my cousin and let her know. I felt like I had to tell someone, and while I was on the phone, who should walk out of the store but my father, so I stood there, watched him walk out of the store and over to his car which was a cheap little Geo Metro, a fact that made me chuckle since my father was always such a car proud man. The last car I had seen him driving was a huge 1979 Ford Thunderbird. And this was not that car. My father retrieved something from inside the car and returned to the store, and as he walked past me, I just continued to talk to my cousin on the telephone. He did pause for a second and look a little closer at me—not a look of recognition, but more of a 'who-the-hell-are-you-stranger' sort of a look—and then he went inside.

"I finished my call and began the six-hour drive to Ohio to see my mother and sisters. The drive was made a little longer, as I kept second guessing my decision and playing the scene over and over in my head. Should I have talked to him? Should I have told him who I was? But, every time I turned it over in my mind, I concluded that I had done the right thing for me, anyway. My mother was of another opinion when I related the story to her. But that was her issue, not my own."

What I think is the most salient part of Eddie's story and the reason I was grateful to be able to include it here is because obviously, in the course of our own experiences of synchronicity and as we read those of others, the improbability of the coincidence is generally the feature that draws our attention. Eddie hadn't been to West Virginia in years and years, and here he was stopping at a small store at the very time that his estranged father was in the back playing checkers and mentioned by name. The unlikelihood of this happening, the perfect timing of it all, jumps out, both to Eddie of course and to us—it feels like an event "meant to be" which it was, in a way, but not because the coincidence became a big, TV-movie style father-and-son reunion. For it wasn't, nor was that what the chance encounter was *meant* to be. Rather, I like Eddie's story a great deal because it shows very clearly that it is up to us to make of the coincidence what *we* will, and what Eddie felt empowered to do in that moment—by sheer chance faced by his dad—was to honor his own feelings about his father and to just keep walking away.

We've heard, thus far, quite a few (and maybe even have even lived some of our own) synchronistic stories of happy, long-sought-after reunions aided by circumstances beyond our control, family connections and reconnections which were surprising and significant because they were welcomed and celebrated. But Eddie helps remind us that our families are also that place in our lives where, for so many of us, all does not always go well, where the bond is one of difficulty, pain, and even estrangement. That, too, is the character of family. Tolstoy's classic beginning of *Anna Karenina* is what comes to mind in this regard: "Happy families are all alike; every unhappy family is unhappy in its own way."

Eddie's father was not a good father. He left and ended his relationship to his wife and his children. And, because of it, because that *was* the character of their relationship—in a word, his father had chosen to have no relationship to either the child or the man Eddie ended up becoming in his life. So, yes, Eddie did in a way experience the startling synchronistic encounter with him so many years later as a sign, but as a sign that having nothing further to do with the man was the right decision. I'm struck by his use of the word "concluded" when he speaks of having turned his decision to say nothing over and over in mind, that he "concluded" he had done the right thing, because the word holds a twin resonance of both resolving a situation and ending a process. It was precisely this conclusion, and the rightness of it, which gave rise to the clearest sign of all, the calm Eddie felt as he left that place. So here is a synchronistic event with an ancestor—in this case, an immediate parent—where the connection is not between two people but rather within oneself. Eddie connected in this event not with his father but rather with himself. It was his own experience of the past and his need to leave behind the anger and pain which the chance encounter helped him affirm for himself.

And Eddie's story, as it turns out, has a bit of a coda, for as he and I worked together in the course of our reviewing and editing his story to appear here in this book, he received word from a relative that his father was gravely ill and then, just as he and I concluding our work together on the story above, he found out that his father Harless Hosey had passed away. As I have come to know, from my work around this phenomenon, the reality of events often has a strangely eerie timeliness to them, and now, here, many months, after he had originally told me his story, he and I conclude the tale of his strained non-relationship with his father with the news of the actual, literal conclusion of his father's life. I asked Eddie what he thought about this criss-crossing of our work and his father's passing, and with characteristic calm, he said to me, that finding out that his father had died "was definitely a non-event and at the same time a relief to know that he is gone. But, it was nice to know that he eventually had a family he could stay with and who loved him."

Another synchronistic encounter from the south, this time from a former psychotherapy client of mine whom I'll call Keith and who was kind enough to give me his consent to use this story, addresses an issue that, for good or for ill, is typically of everyone's family dynamics, namely, family secrets. Many times, finding an appropriate title for a book such as this one can be a bit of a fraught process—you want the title to be faithful to what the book is about, but you also want the title to grab a bit of the reader's attention. *There Are No Accidents* was good for getting a little bit of a rise out of the synchronicity skeptics— "accidents do happen!" they all wanted to say when seeing that particular title—and though I like *Unexpected Pieces of Our Hearts*, one of the titles that was suggested to me for this book was *Secrets of Synchronicity: Stories From Our Families*. Had I gone with that title, Keith's story would have fit in perfectly. Here's what happened to him.

"As far as I knew at the time this strange coincidence happened to me, I had grown up in a completely normal family in a relatively normal neighborhood in Austin, Texas. My mom was a stay-at-home mom, my dad had a regular steady job. Austin's the state capital, but it has its own particular character, progressive, musical, not a typical Texas town, according to what people generally think of as Texas. I had a younger sister and we got along just fine. We were close to my dad's relatives more than my mom's, but I really didn't make much of that because my dad's parents were still alive, whereas my mom's folks had passed away before I came along and, as far as I knew, she had been an only child. The one thing, looking back, that was a little out of the ordinary was that I realized, at about elementary school age, that my parents were a little older than my friends' parents. This is the South, people tend to have their families early, so my friends' parents are in their late 20s, while my dad and mom are in their 40s. There was a moment in 3rd grade, I think, when I realized that my dad was actually a good deal older than my teacher, and you know when you are young, you think of your teachers as really old, even though some of them were just out of college themselves. Which made my own father, I realized, really *really* old. So that was a little unusual, but as I said, otherwise everything was just pretty normal for me.

"I graduate high school just fine, I go to school at the University of Texas, Austin, again, all according to plan, and after college, I get a job in the field of marketing, starting at this entry level position in a media marketing firm, which means that I'm the one they are sending out on the road a lot. And I mean, a *lot*. Texas is a big place, I have this enormous territory, there's a whole commission structure to the salary I'm being paid, so selling advertising to businesses is how I make my living, and being honest, I wouldn't say it was my most ideal job, because I'm on the road literally like four to five days a week. But on the other hand, I was young, very unattached, didn't really mind driving, and I did like the independence of it and the possibility of the sky being the limit in terms of what I could make. If I was good at my sales, then I saw the result in my pocket, and I did like that.

"So, in my first year, I'm not doing too bad. I had inherited the territory from a previous starter who had moved up in the company, and like I said, it was a big territory to cover, so most of the first year, I'm just traveling all over, making the contacts, working the sales. That's when one week, I'm on my way out to a sales call, heading out of Austin to the west, which is not usually the way I have to go, and this is all before Google Maps and GPS and such, so I get kinda lost on these little country roads going through these little towns, and my car over-heats. So, I manage to make it to this town, Brookside, and I get the car to a garage that happens to be open. It's a pain in the neck, sure, but it's nothing really life-threatening or weird, just a busted hose, they have to get a hold of one, they'll have one in an hour or two, so I'm in Brookside, cooling my heels.

"It's lunchtime, I decide to walk down to this roadside diner, which is really like the only place in town. I sit down, things are good, I order, and that's when I notice this lady behind the counter working there, and she's sorta staring at me. I'm just thinking that I probably stick out like a sore thumb in this little town where I'm sure no one ever comes by, but then I look back at her, and it hits me that she looks a lot like my mama, a little younger, a little thinner, but there's something really interesting about her eyes and the shape of her face. Anyway, she looks at me, I look at her, and by the end of the lunch, when I go up to pay the check, I say to her, 'Good afternoon, have we met? You look a little familiar to me.' She shrugs her shoulders and smiles a little, and says something like, 'We don't get many strangers in here. I'm sorry if I was staring.' Waiting for my change, I say that I'm from Austin, the car broke down, and she stares again in that peculiar sort of way. "Austin, huh?" And that's all she says.

"I really didn't think much of it at all at the time, and I had a pretty busy life during that period so it wasn't until a long time, probably a couple of months later, that I was over my folks' house for dinner, barbecue, something, and I go into the house to go to the bathroom, and there on the kitchen table on the side is all their mail, right, in a big pile and there I see this card for my mama, you know, like a greeting card, unopened but the return address is an address in Brookside and it's handwritten. And I probably wouldn't have even noticed that, I mean, my mother knew a lot of people, except for the fact that my car had broken down those months before in Brookside, and I had had to hang out there that afternoon while it got fixed. So, I go back out to the patio after I go to the bathroom and say to my mama, 'Who do you know in Brookside? I saw you got a card in there from Brookside, and my car broke down there a couple of months ago in the middle of a sales call and I had to spend the afternoon there. Kind of in the middle of nowhere.' So that's when my mama gets this weird look on her face, she looks at my daddy, daddy looks at mama and she says something like it's an old girlfriend of hers sending her a belated birthday card or something. And even then, I don't even think about it. I'm like 22 years old at the time and I'm in my own world, you know, so we have our barbecue, move on.

"Until about a week later, when I get a call from my daddy and he says he and Mama want me to come over, and when I do, I can tell it's a big deal. Mama looks like she's been crying, and that's when they tell me. It turns out that the woman I grew up thinking was my mother, my mama, was actually not my biological mother, but in fact is my aunt. My real mama, my biological mother, was her younger sister, who had me when she was really young and not married. But that was the first year my parents were married, so they took me after my real mama gave birth, legally adopted me and raised me.

"I felt really, really bad for my parents, because I could just tell how torn apart they were, apologizing over and over for not having told me earlier, they kept meaning to, never found the right time to, didn't want to upset me, every time they thought they would something came up, someone got sick, something happened. At which point then Mama said, 'And when I heard you were in Brookside, and you saw that card,

I knew we had to do it, because your real mama, my sister lives there, and that card was her sending me a note saying that she thought she saw you there one day, and asking me was it you.'

"She was, like I said, very emotional, and said, 'And I couldn't figure out how I was going to ask you if you had been there, and your daddy and I talked and talked and talked about it until finally he said, you know, baby, we just gotta tell him. Your mama has felt bad for 22 years that she hasn't been able to be a mama to you, and she didn't want anyone in that town to know what she had done, so she really has stayed away because of that, not because she didn't love you. She knew you were happy here, and she didn't want to mess anything up, but when you ended up in Brookside that day and she thought she saw you in that restaurant, she didn't even dare to call here, in case you answered, so she sent that note and asked me if that was you. And that's when you told us, without knowing what you were saying, that yes, it was you."

"So that's how I found out the truth about the whole family secret they had been keeping, and it was pretty hard for a long time for me, I'm not going to lie. As much as I love my parents, who I now call my aunt and uncle which is what they actually are, I was pretty angry that they didn't really tell me the truth, and if my car hadn't broken down, and I hadn't eaten at that place in Brookside, I don't think they would have told me. It wasn't long after that when I did go back to meet my real mother and it was a little awkward, I have to tell the truth about that, too. I guess she had been really young, I mean, *really* young, like 14 when she had me, and I could just tell that the experience was very, very hard on her. It's small-town Texas out there, even though it really isn't that far from big-city Austin, and without parents of her own, the arrangement my aunt and she made to give me up and make it look like I was my aunt and uncle's baby in a way makes sense, and I can say I had a very stable childhood because of it.

"But the thing of it for me was that in the end it wasn't the truth, it wasn't my truth, and I was really angry about that for a long time.

160

Not so much anymore, because I've mellowed with age and I see how complicated things are in life. But still, hell of a chance to cross paths with your birth mother because your car breaks down. I'm just glad now how it put pressure on my aunt and uncle to finally do the right thing by me, which they did, and they didn't have to, really, they could have kept the pretense up. But the coincidence was a little bit of a sign to them, I think, that they couldn't continue to be doing that. I also think my birth mother seeing me made her realize that she couldn't just pretend it was OK with her for the rest of her life. So that's how that particular set of circumstances put an end to a very long-standing family secret for me and for the rest of us. Things are better now the truth's out, definitely better for me. It's like I know who I really am and where I stand in the world."

Keith's story exemplifies many lessons that I myself have learned and been witness to others learning in the course of my long practice as a family counselor. The first and most prominent is that so-called family secrets rarely stay secret. In line with that humorous observation that three people can keep a secret, as long as two of them are dead, I have seen countless times now that this observation is even more true with families. Someone has knowledge of what happened, and no matter how great their determination, how noble their motivations, how comprehensively they go about hiding, masking or even outright lying, the truth about what happened—the sexual abuse, the alcoholism, the accident, or, say in this case, Keith's mother's youthful, unplanned pregnancy—will come out sooner or later.

Why is this? One can posit a number of reasons for the primacy of the truth and its implacable tendency to surface in all its complex difficulty, but in keeping with the psychology of the unconscious put forward by Jung, I would say that the archetype of the Self, that powerful natural inward force each of us possesses that moves us inexorably toward an ideal state of wholeness, is what is responsible inside each of us for our eventually, almost irresistibly, stepping forward and speaking the truth. And, again psychologically speaking, insofar as the family itself exemplifies the archetype of the Self, providing each of us with a particular kind of paradigm emotionally in which the family represents integration, safety and completeness, then the archetype of the Self is most certainly what drives individual members of a family system to reveal whatever deep dark secret they have been hiding about the past, about themselves, or about events concerning the family as a whole.

It may be that I am somewhat biased as a family counselor about this matter, since after all, I see individual, couples, and families almost exclusively in the midst of a process in which they are needing assistance toward a greater level of integration and wholeness, so naturally, it is more often the case than not that I get the phone call to start counseling following a blockbuster revelation—the affair has been discovered, the mismanagement of the family's finances has been exposed, someone's long-hidden drug problem or sexual fetish is now out in the open. So, with every passing year, it seems more and more true to me that trying to keep a secret within a family is a losing proposition over the long-term. If someone knows, then eventually everyone will know, and usually, following the course of such a revelation, the individuals I work with come to see the wisdom and truth of simply being honest from the start, radically honest, no matter how difficult or painful or humiliating the truth may be about who they are, what they have done or what happened. We tend to blithely say, "honesty is the best policy," which is certainly true, but I have come to see the truth as a vastly more powerful force than a mere policy. Because it is a psychological necessity for integration, it will not and cannot be denied in perpetuity, and the sheer unconscious power of its suppression within the dense network of psychic energy that is any family system means that sooner or later, next year, next decade, or even in the next generation, the truth will be known.

So that is the context in which I would like to place Keith's experience here, because although the somewhat unlikely and entirely accidental circumstances of the events are, naturally, what draw our attention—that his car would break down in the very town where his birth mother was living, that he would physically cross paths with her in the diner, and then subsequently come across her note to her sister, his mother, many weeks later—I think the unlikelihood of it all needs to be seen within the ambit of how much pressure this long-held family secret was actually placing on his parents who were raising their nephew as their son and on his birth mother herself who knew she was still living in the same geographical area as her son and knew exactly at any point where she could find him, if she so desired. So, while for Keith himself, the most unwitting of the situation, the synchronicity was beyond startling, if we draw back, look upon the whole situation and take into account what his parents confessed to during their eventual revelation—how ardently they felt it was that they tell him about his origins, how heart-rending it was for them for him not to know and for them to persistently not find the right time—then we see a level of unconscious feeling at work in his family which, I believe, would have occasioned this kind of revelation eventually anyway.

In other words, synchronicity might seem mystical, shocking, even far-fetched, but if we adopt the psychological lens to examine a given incident, we see an underlying wholeness to who we are, an underlying unity to our family experience, a rich coming together of emotional and social ties, that makes sense of these sorts of meaningful coincidences. Of course, Keith would find out about his origins. Of course, the circumstances would present themselves to his parents. Of course, his mother would eventually find her child. The only element that makes it synchronistic is that the closing of the circle happened by way of chance rather than by conscious intention.

And Keith's story also is like Eddie's and in some ways like many of the stories in this book, in that someone rather unacquainted with the full nature of synchronistic events or their psychological basis might expect that the conclusion of these tales would be "happy ever after." Who wouldn't want that to be the case, but here we see in these real stories that life is not a fairy tale, and that there is always a double edge, particularly on the emotional level, when a family moves forward to greater integration. Sometimes the conclusion, like Eddie's, is to keep the door to the past closed, and sometimes, like Keith, that door gets opened and there is no closing it again, despite the disruption. But in both cases, resolution requires everyone concerned to expand their capacity for feeling and holding conflictual emotional states simultaneously.

Jung famously said that he considered original sin to be one-sidedness, by which he meant that the source of evil in the world was our psychological tendency to cling to what we find pleasant and acceptable and to repress, deny or persecute that which we find un-pleasant or objectionable, both in ourselves and in projected form onto others. James Hillman, well-known Jungian analyst, echoed this view when he said the two cardinal rules of analysis, if it were to effect psychological healing, were contradictory: don't repress—feel every-thing fully and completely—but don't act out—hold those feelings fully and completely without allowing them to be discharged in action. Maybe a slightly less abstruse way to say this would be to note that our wholeness is not a state of blissful peace devoid of conflict but rather more the opposite, a state of stable but dynamic tension between con-flicting views, feelings and impulses all of which we feel fully and hold effectively together in ourselves without blaming, avoiding, or absolving ourselves of responsibility.

Indeed, many of us seek happiness and perhaps dream of a para-dise free from care. Meanwhile on earth, among the mortals, we see a different sort of wholeness, the kind of integration that Keith and Eddie did achieve for themselves in the course of their own family experience which has both dark and light aspects to it—relief and freedom but also grief and anger; clarity and certainty, but also conflict and sadness. And in a way, I wonder to myself, how could it be otherwise in our families, particularly given the theme of this chapter's exploration, in which the past and present, what's lost and what is found, get woven together into a fabric of meaning that circles around attachment and loss.

In addressing the synchronistic connections we have with our ancestors, of course, one of the drawbacks is that our forebears aren't around to give us their side of the story; but indeed, as we have seen in other stories, a synchronistic event for one person may not necessarily be for another. Nor is every meaningful coincidence something that happens in a flash. My friend Karen Erlichman's rather amazing story of how, by complete and utter chance, her father and her brother came upon information that connected them with a tragic past they thought they might never fully know about, no less find a way to heal. This is an example of how sometimes many, many years go by before the synchronistic ties we have to those who have gone before becomes manifest. I was lucky enough to have all three of them tell me their family's remarkable story.

Karen begins by giving us the overview. "In the spring of 2006, my brother Billy and my father Roy went on a trip to Israel. They had not traveled together as father and son since Billy was a kid. My father said he had been feeling spiritually empty and was hoping this trip would be more of a soul pilgrimage. For my own part, I was excited for them; but I don't mind admitting, I was also a little worried that they might get swooped up by the ultra-Orthodox while they were there and become "ba'al teshuvah" (which translates as "master of the answer")—or, more colloquially, "spiritual know-it-alls."

"While there, among the many sites they visited was Yad VaShem, the World Holocaust Remembrance Center. As you might expect, at Yad VaShem there is a Reference and Information Services department which maintains a vast database that includes not only names of those who were murdered in the Holocaust, but also communication from those who survived and are seeking contact with other family members.

"So, as my dad and brother were perusing the database, they came upon one form that had been completed in Spanish, written by a woman named Ela Erlichman. Curiously, my father, who is Jewish and from Philadelphia, is completely fluent in Spanish, because of a whole series of life circumstances that aren't entirely relevant to this story. My brother is also fluent in Spanish, so when this form popped up in Spanish, Dad didn't even blink because he could read and understand it completely. Synchronicity number one, here. Spanish form, Dad finds it in Israel and can actually read it.

"But then there's the story itself. As my father read the entry at Yad Vashem , Ela Erlichman and her family were in Romania during the Second World War, and he learned they were ultimately captured by the Nazis and sent to a concentration camp in the Ukraine, where they spent five brutal years. One sister and brother died there in the camp in approximately 1943. When the war ended and the camps were liberated, Ela and her remaining sister were the only surviving family members. At that point, they went on a bit of odyssey, first traveling to Transylvania, then to Palestine, and finally to Lima, Peru where they ultimately settled and raised her family. There it was that Ela met her husband, and they had two sons, Moishe and Saul. Their son Saul grew up and married a woman from Ecuador and moved to Guayaquil, where they had two children, Alex and Valerie. Moishe, the other son, remained in Lima, had one son himself named Daniel, but was subsequently divorced and moved in with Ela to care for her in her later years of life. As we were to find out, and as you might imagine, the Jewish community in Lima is quite small and includes a fair number of Holocaust survivor families and their offspring.

"We were all stunned but, of course, quite thrilled that this completely chance discovery at Yad VaShem had given us access to a part of our family's past that we might never have otherwise had. A full year of email correspondence then ensued between Moishe, my father and brother, the three of them piecing together the torn patchwork of our family history. We three had known that my father's grandfather's family, more specifically my great-grandfather's side of the family, was originally from Romania and Russia, but at the point in which my father came across this information about Ela, my great-grandfather and all of his siblings had long since died, along with any of the historical information they had. But as we were to find out, by an extraordinarily fortunate chance, the past and the present would not be kept apart.

"After a year of email, in January 2007, Ela and Moishe invited my father and stepmother to Lima, and though we could not be certain, we were 99% sure of our family connection. Yet, perhaps more compelling was our shared feeling of *bashert,* a Yiddish word meaning "destiny." It felt like it had been meant for us to know one another, so Dad made the travel arrangements and invited me to join them. That June, my father, stepmother and I traveled to Lima. The flight was a little more than five hours long. Our plane landed after midnight, and we were jittery with fatigue and anticipation as we followed the lines through customs. There was a waiting area outside where people gathered to greet those arriving at the airport. At that time of year, the weather in Lima is similar to San Francisco, cool and foggy. The night air was thick with fog. We squinted into the crowd looking for someone we had never seen before, until we laid eyes on Moishe who, as I remember it, was utterly radiant, almost as if a beam of light were shining on him. Greeting us with open arms and a big, open heart which we would learn was the hallmark of his *neshama* or soul, we hugged and kissed and spoke to each other in a jumbled mixture of Spanish, Yiddish and English.

To say that Moishe and Ela were hospitable and solicitous would be an enormous understatement. They took us to see the sights and wonders of Lima, including the small Jewish community, local kosher market (complete with *mikveh* or ritual bath right in the market!); that Friday night, we shared an entirely magical Shabbat dinner together with these long-separated loved ones. Ela herself must have spent the entire day preparing the Shabbat meal, everything homemade from scratch, Ashkenazi style. She also brought out a bottle of sweet wine, and told us she had made the wine herself almost twenty years ago and was saving it for an unknown special occasion. This reunion was that special occasion. After dinner, we went to Friday night services with Ela and Moishe at the Orthodox synagogue in Lima. Instead of a traditional *mechitzah*, the ritual divider separating the men from the women, the men's section there was in the center and the women sat separately on the sides. So, I sat next to Ela and can still remember how it felt to be next to her and to hear her sing and chant in Hebrew, our shared language of prayer. That evening something felt completed in me, something that all of the tragedy of the past could not keep us from living together again."

Luckily for me, both Karen's dad Roy and her brother Billy were willing to share their sides of this reunion story, which make clear from the details of their experience, how apt the term *bashert* really is: a coming together that feels as if it were indeed meant to be.

Roy shared a bit of the personal context for him in his life. "I have had a lifelong inner struggle to understand universal questions, and I would say this internal seeking began well before my bar mitzvah. My academic studies were traditional coursework, but individual tutorials over four years in college with three ministers in particular stirred further questions for me in this regard that remained unanswered. I was introduced to Heschel, Niebuhr, Buber, Kierkegaard, among others, which ultimately led to my ongoing direct study sessions with Rabbi Heschel at Jewish Theological Seminary in New York. With Rabbi Heschel, I finally found a place and a mentor with whom to explore my questions, but nonetheless, my inner wrestling has persisted throughout my life. When younger, I dismissed organized Judaism but still felt the tug and intrigue of the traditional. As my career turned a corner and I pursued psychoanalytic training, I had even more difficulty reconciling science and psychoanalysis. It was tangible truth I sought, proof, but I was to find again and again there was none.

"So then, little more than ten years ago, my son Billy gave me the gift of a trip to Israel with him. Seeing Israel with my own eyes was indescribably meaningful. Yet, as we went through the trip, I was very aware that here, too, there seemed to be no burning bush for me, no moment of definite revelation, that was, until our visit to Yad Vashem."

At this point Billy, Roy's son and Karen's brother, jumps in to give us his perspective on the journey.

"I think I need to say that, really, for the bulk of our trip to Israel, Dad ignored God. That's how I would put it. He would not put prayer notes in the Wall, you know, the so-called Wailing Wall, the remnant of the last temple of Jerusalem where the faithful go for prayers. It seemed he really wouldn't touch the innards of his own spirituality. For my dad—typically—everything was more historic, academic, analytical, so his experience was understandably more intellectual than spiritual up to that point. Dad often goes back to his 'God in Search of Man vs. Man in Search of God' debate which always and ultimately led to a non-resolution that was more aligned with cultural affinity free of spiritual affinity. For me, the experience was very different. Whereas I could feel the presence of God in the breathing of the wall, Dad would see the architecture and the history *of* the wall, not what lived *inside* those magnificently crafted boulders. I felt the cry of our people during my time on the land whereas Dad felt the awe of ancient storytelling and history. At the Dead Sea, for example, he would not go in the water. At Masada, which was in fact one of his favorite moments, he reveled in its history but did not appear to feel the miraculously ordained character of the self-sacrifice that occurred in that place. For him, it was very meaningful, but it was not spiritual. But then, as he said, he went to Yad Vashem."

Billy continues, and the emotion in his story is palpable. "The weight of the experience at Yad Vashem is indescribable. Walking through the building, every corner, every image, every story knocks on the door of the human conscience. One cannot endure that memorial museum and not be overwhelmed by a tidal wave of humility, horror, emotion, and—for Jews—an extraordinary sadness. As a people, for the thousands of years of our history, we have been targeted, whether as slaves or as Nobel prize winners. It makes no difference, and, in today's modern age, as the Holocaust fades with the dying of the last survivors, we ask ourselves: how do we move forward while not forgetting? That question is the conundrum that we face as people nowadays and, sadly, tragically, as soon as we start forgetting the last time we were so persecuted, then the next persecution somehow seems to manifest itself.

"At Yad Vashem, I could tell that the horrors documented in the museum were a lot for Dad to take in and that he was doing all he could to resist going down the emotional rabbit hole of injustice. Unlike with my sister, to whom he shows a more emotional side, with me, his son, my Dad is typically male and fights to bite his upper lip, and as it happens, I am the same with my kids, so I don't blame him. I understand it. Plus, the Holocaust is too much for anyone to bear, and if anything, I would say Yad Vashem only further solidified his belief that Israel was historically important and culturally meaningful but not so much a spiritual force. For after all, if you look at it logically as my dad would, logic dictates that any just God would not allow for such an unjust series of events.

"So, all of that is happening within him and within me, so by the end of the tour, we were walking through and not pausing to take in all of the images. Truly, it was overwhelming, and I think we both needed some fresh air. However, before we left, it turned out, there was a database for Holocaust survivors, funded by Steve Spielberg, open to all for research on their families' histories, housed in a relatively sterile room that looked like the business center at a Hyatt hotel—nothing fancy, a couple of computers and a laser printer in dark wood cubicles, as I recall, with a bunch of hospital waiting room type furniture and an easy prompt-clear computer program so you could enter your family's name and see if any relatives appeared. I suggested we try.

"At first, I vaguely recall typing in Yanowich—my maternal grandfather's name—and many names came up, but nothing that resonated with me as it relates to connecting to Poppy. I remember I tried Bloom—my paternal grandmother's name—and again there were so many names, so then I tried Biloon, and once again, a bunch of hits, but no real connection. At that point, I thought to myself, 'Let's type Erlichman.'

"So I did. And waited. At which point, up popped on the screen I saw a black and white photograph of a little girl that looked like my sister Karen. Big eyes, dark hair, our family coloring. Now *that* picture called out to me, and as I stared at the screen, I tried to remember my uncle's middle name.' David.

"And there it was. On the screen, Ela and David Erlichman. With this picture of Ela, or maybe Leah, her sister; I'm not sure. Either way, it looked just like Karen, my sister. I was breathless. All I remember thinking is that I wanted my dad to see it, and to see how he would react. So, I printed the document in the printer nearby the computer, the picture, along with a description of our relatives who fled Romania and ultimately wound up in Peru.

"I will never forget Dad holding the piece of paper and his hand started to tremble a bit. He began to whisper over and over. 'Oh my. Oh my. Oh my.'

"It's very difficult to describe how I felt observing my father trying to reconcile his own emotions in the moment. The best I can say was that it was like watching the water in his body rise very quickly above his shoulders, above his chin, above his nose, until his eyes started to well up with the rising tide. And the first thing he said to me was, 'I have to call my brother.'

"Now, my uncle Eliot has since died, but when he passed, the moment that immediately came to my mind was this one, at Yad Vashem, and it still does, to this day, whenever I think of the braided bond between my father and his brother.

"So there, in Israel, right away we walked outside so that he could call Uncle Eliot on his cell phone. And I could see he was sad but also happy because Ela was alive, and immediately I knew that making contact would be an inevitability. I'll let my dad fill in the rest of the story, but I do want to say that for my father, right there, I could see he would never be the same. So later that day, as we were in Jerusalem, I thought we should return to the wall, since we were leaving the next day. Only this time, Dad went to the Wall alone, and this time with a yarmulke on his head. And there, from a distance, I watched him in that familiar posture, his hand on the wall, his shoulders gently bouncing with humility. No, then I knew. He would never be the same. None of us would."

Roy continues the story of his experience from that moment and reflects on the rather startling synchronistic connections the information brought to his awareness, connections that began that day and continued on in the entire series of life-changing events that grew out of that chance discovery.

"After wandering independently through the memorial which is quite extensive, as Billy just told you, it so happened Billy 'chose' to look up our name Erlichman in the Yad Vashem database, and what appeared—or I might say, was revealed to us—were forms prepared by Ela Erlichman along with her sisters and her brother David. Looking for family. Note their names: Ela and David Erlichman. My brother's name is Eliot David Erlichman.

"I knew virtually nothing about my own family history. I recalled a random comment my father had made, after meeting some Erlichmans from Montreal, when he said that we were probably related, if these Erlichmans originally came from Romania and Russia. Here, at Yad Vashem, Billy and I saw that Ela's family was in fact, from both Romania and Russia.

"And, as my son and daughter have said, there was a further confirmation, because the Yad Vashem document we had before us was in Spanish, the only language we speak besides English. That was the moment when all the roads we traveled pointed to Peru or Ecuador, where the Felmans, specifically the second of Ela's sons and his family, lived.

"When I got home from Israel, I recounted this story to one of my daughters-in-law, Ivana, and it turned out her mother 'coincidentally' was going to Lima *the very next day*. So again, 'coincidentally,' her mother went about finding the Felmans while she was traveling. Valerie, Ela's granddaughter, just happened to be visiting her grandmother in Lima at that time. Ivana's mother met the family and Valerie was there to translate, and to explain what Billy and I had discovered in the Yad VaShem documents in Israel.

"Shortly thereafter, my wife Gail and I were at the Colombia Restaurant in West Palm Beach, having dinner with our friends Naomi and Alan Berger. Naomi is the daughter of Auschwitz survivors and grew up in Netanya, Israel. Alan is a world-renowned expert on the Holocaust and distinguished professor at Florida Atlantic University. They had met years before at Hebrew University in Jerusalem. At dinner, Gail and I are telling the Bergers about the Peru family and the extraordinary confluence of events that began at Yad Vashem—and of course, we mention that we are seriously considering going there to visit Ela and Moishe. However, we didn't know anything about Peru, let alone how to best travel there. As it happened that night, our server at that restaurant was a very personable young man named Franco. Without thinking, and with no knowledge of Franco—we had never met or spoken—I somehow 'knew' without question that he was from

Lima. When he returned to the table, I simply asked him, "Franco, where are you from?" to which he answered, "Lima, Peru." I then asked him if he flew to Lima from Miami—and he answered, 'yes, I do'—and I asked him how long the flight was. Needless to say, we were all flabbergasted at this 'coincidental' interchange.

"Now another aspect of this story is the curious connection to Ecuador, but I did not know why until later I learned that Moishe's brother Saul lived in Guayaquil, Ecuador, a small community with about 70 Jewish families. Heretofore Ecuador had been simply a name on the map of South America. But once we discovered that Ela's son Saul lived there, we began to meet people from Ecuador, and specifically Guayaquil. For example, one day, Gail and I stopped at the local branch of our bank to take care of some business, and I needed to talk with the bank officer who was a charming young woman named Paola. I heard her speaking and started to speak to her in Spanish. I think my wife Gail was about to ask her where she was from since her Spanish was not the local *dialect*. I quickly intervened and asked if she was from Guayaquil, to which she answered with a very surprised "Yes!" Of course, I had no way of knowing this. I had no idea what Ecuadorean Spanish sounded like and had never met a person from Ecuador, let alone Guayaquil. Thereafter any number of people from Ecuador crossed my path. *Coincidencia pura? Creo que no.*

"Still more connections began to happen. My son Billy had hired an intern at his company, a young man named Jeffrey Fischman, who turned out to be a musician from Lima, Peru. A friend of Billy's had introduced Jeffrey to Billy long before the trip to Lima was even planned. It turned out that Jeffrey Fischman from Lima actually knew the Erlichmans of Lima from our family, because the Lima Jewish community is very small, and they were all members of the same synagogue.

"After some writing back and forth, we decided to go to Lima at the invitation of Moishe and Ela. It was deeply meaningful, and the experience transcended language. When we returned to the United States, we showed my elderly mom many beautiful photographs we had taken in Peru with our family. When she saw the photo of Saul, she exclaimed, 'I did not realize that (your brother) Eliot went on the trip with you!' My brother Eliot actually had not gone with us, but he and Saul looked so much alike that even my mother mistook Saul from Ecuador for her own son Eliot.

"These kinds of coincidences did not stop. About five years later, Gail and I traveled to Israel for a vacation. After arriving on the first day, we were tired but decided to take a walk in the neighborhood surrounding the hotel. We stopped to admire several beautiful sculptures on the walking path, and stopped to admire a particular bronze sculpture made by…Yael Erlichman, of all names. We were astonished.

"On that same trip, Gail and I went together to Yad Vashem. After two hours or more in Yad Vashem, I really did not want to go to the Children's Memorial but our guide Doron insisted. Had we not stopped for those few minutes of discussion with our guide, we would have missed hearing the names, ages and countries of children on the loud speaker, particularly "Leah Erlichman, Age 15, Romania," on the loud-speaker. Stunned!"

"Since the reunion, we maintained contact with Ela and Moishe, sending emails and a few occasional phone calls. Moishe ended up being diagnosed with leukemia and a cardiac complication. He only lived for a short time after our trip to Lima. His premature death was heartbreaking for all of us. I thought then and think now that had Billy not discovered Ela Erlichman's document at Yad Vashem, we would not have known him or the family. Events aligned mysteriously. The sheer quality of these seeming coincidences defied logic and possibility."

To conclude, I asked Karen to reflect on this story with me. She echoed some of what Billy her brother had said to me, "Few adult children have the privilege of invitation to bear witness to a parent's spiritual journey. My brother and I continue to walk this path with our father, accompanied by the courageous guidance of our ancestors and family members who have since passed on to *Olam haBah*, that is 'the World to Come.' It has been a deeply moving and inspiring experience. We have a prayer in our tradition, the *Tefilat ha'Derech*, the Traveler's Prayer, that for me remains the best response to what we have been given:

May it be Your will, our God and God of our ancestors,
that You guide us in peace and help us reach our destination
safely, joyfully and peacefully.
May You protect us on our leaving and on our return,
and rescue us from any harm,
and may You bless the work of our hands,
May we find grace, love and compassion in Your sight
And in the sight of all who see us.
Hear our plea, for You listen to prayer and supplication.
Blessed are You, Source of All, who hears our prayer.

CHAPTER FIVE

Stop All The Clocks: Synchronicity and Completion of Life

Jung thought of the psyche as a natural phenomenon and a self-regulating system, not unlike our physical bodies. If a situation of illness or infection or stress occurs, our bodies react—the immune system rears up, antibodies and white blood cells get activated, our temperature rises, hormones and chemicals are secreted—all focused on repairing, restabilizing, restoring the smooth, healthy functioning we had before the pathogen or the stress disrupted our physical well-being.

Likewise, thought Jung, with our psychological health: when the inner world of our emotional life is disrupted—by trauma or stress—our psyche reacts by bringing imagery, experiences, feelings, and symbols from the level of our unconscious experience into our conscious awareness, all of which are intended to repair, restabilize and restore our sense of integration and groundedness inwardly and outwardly. This compensatory action of the unconscious, as Jung termed it, and its consistent role in maintaining our psychological sense of well-being despite the vicissitudes of life led him to appreciate, and indeed, as a clinician, to count on assistance from the unconscious in moving his patients toward health and wholeness, no matter how dark or difficult the situation we find ourselves in.

And of all situations we face in this life, none is more dark, difficult and singularly disruptive as death. As a species and as individuals, our attachment to others is the original source of our actual literal physical lives—each of us comes into being through a union of two people—and so throughout all our lives, intimate relationships

177

continue provide the sustenance which enables us to survive and thrive. Without relationship, we simply cannot be. So, when death presents us with the definitive and inevitable rupture of relationship—from those we love, certainly, but in the end, of course, from our very own body itself—our psyche, all our psyches, come up against a universal and, ultimately, unfathomable transition. From mortality, not one of us is spared, and what it means to leave this life has yet to be fully revealed to any of us. That is the nature of death: it has been and always will be the final mystery.

> Stop all the clocks, cut off the telephone,
> Prevent the dog from barking with a juicy bone,
> Silence the pianos and with muffled drum
> Bring out the coffin, let the mourners come.
>
> Let aeroplanes circle moaning overhead
> Scribbling on the sky the message He Is Dead,
> Put crepe bows round the white necks of the public doves,
> Let the traffic policemen wear black cotton gloves.
>
> He was my North, my South, my East and West,
> My working week and my Sunday rest,
> My noon, my midnight, my talk, my song;
> I thought that love would last for ever: I was wrong.
>
> The stars are not wanted now: put out every one;
> Pack up the moon and dismantle the sun;
> Pour away the ocean and sweep up the wood.
> For nothing now can ever come to any good. (W. H. Auden,
> "Twelve Songs: IX, Funeral Blues," *W. H. Auden Collected Poems*. New York: Random House, 1940/1968.

As Auden's well-known poem describes so movingly, the rich life of our unconscious often reacts to death by offering synchronistic events up to our attention. Clocks stop. The music goes silent. Events in the external world reflect back to us—if we are looking, if we are open to it—the inward grief and loss we feel. As if to compensate the disruptive and disintegrative effect of death on our lives and our sense of coherence, meaningful coincidences sometimes seem to suddenly crowd about us, acting almost as if to *prepare* us for the experience of death. At times, such events can be strikingly premonitory coincidences that halt us in our tracks and really force us to pay attention to the loss we are facing: I recall the various incidents Jung reported about his own family members' near-death experiences from his autobiography, his grandson's near drowning, his dream of his deceased sister accompanying a close friend who, he discovered upon waking, had passed away that night. And sometimes, the synchronistic event is not especially dramatic. My good friend Chris, with whom I was talking as I was writing this chapter, somewhat matter-of-factly said to me, "Well, you know, I knew one or two days before I actually received the phone call from my mother that my grandmother had died. I still see very clearly where I was—I was in my apartment in Seattle, it was around 5:00 p.m. in the afternoon. And really, I was not thinking specifically about her, I didn't have any reason to, when suddenly I just simply had the thought: 'Oh! Nonnie just died.'"

I raised my eyebrows and in typical form for the deeply spiritual, introverted, intuitive person he was, Chris calmly explained to me. "Truth be told, even then I didn't feel the need to call home to confirm, I was that confident in my knowledge. I just simply *knew*. And because I was in the midst of preparations for a retreat that I was going to be leading, I just assumed that my mother would call me with the news at some point. So, when she did, a couple of days later, I didn't want to tell her that Nonnie's death actually wasn't 'news' to me. I didn't want to scare her!"

In situations where our defenses, denial and unconsciousness about the impending death are substantial and strong, or when perhaps the death is unexpected and sudden, I've noticed that the synchronistic events can be sometimes quite dramatic and attention-grabbing—dreams you can't forget, coincidences you can't ignore. And yes, these do make for some great family stories. My grandmother often told the tale of her own mother's unexpected death the week after a bird had flown through an open window into her mother's bedroom, triggering a great deal of anxiety on everyone's part, as it seems there is a long-standing German superstition that a bird flying inside the house is a presage of death. For her, the events were connected. "It was a sign," she would tell us kids, with a serious face and a single raised finger.

But sometimes, as with Jung or my friend Chris, if we live our lives with a level of openness and awareness, preparatory synchronicities can be much subtler—a series of experiences that only afterward, we see, came together and quietly, persistently, readied us to face a loss.

The synchronistic experiences I had during my own husband's last year of life were actually a little of both—at first intriguing, but also, with time, becoming more and more dramatic. It all began with simply one little oddity. Once Paul's Alzheimer's progressed to late-stage and qualified him medically to be place into a skilled nursing facility, I took the first couple of months of relative freedom from his daily caretaking to finally attend to the long list of deferred home maintenance projects that I hadn't the time or the energy to do before. One of those was replacing our old, broken doorbell with a new wireless one. Pretty easy. But a couple of months after continuous, reliable functioning, it began, quite unaccountably, to ring—only when I got to the door, no one was there. I didn't think much of it at first, though it was disconcerting to jump up, get to the door and find the porch empty. And as it continued to happen, even though I checked the device, replaced the batteries, read the instructions again to make sure I'd set it up right, it began to become a little eerie, so eerie, in fact, that I began keeping an actual written list of dates and times when it was happening. Eventually, as the months went on and I logged dozens of incidents, I realized, even more weirdly, that it only rang like this between 2 and 4 in the afternoon, but because it was wireless and the window of time was so specific, I soon started to think that someone's car clicker or TV remote nearby was setting it off. Maybe a neighbor coming home from work around that time every day and clicking his car lock or someone watching their favorite program in the afternoon, switching on their remote: their errant signal ringing my wonky doorbell. However, little did I realize at the time that this was only the first of many electricity-related synchronicities that were to occur throughout this period.

As Paul's decline continued, one day in September his hospice nurse called me, sounding professional but nevertheless somewhat alarmed, to let me know that she had discovered during her regular weekly visit that his breathing had shifted to a pattern that, she felt, indicated he may not have much longer to live—long periods of apnea—sometimes not breathing for over a minute—then followed by slower and slower respiration. I went to the nursing home immediately that day, expecting the worst—only to find him up and about in his walker, roaming the hallways. So, I stayed through dinner, made sure he was put in bed for the night, and went home somewhat later than usual, around 9:30 p.m.

That night, at home, I was sitting in my living room, scrolling through Facebook on my iPod, thinking about what kind of post to write about this latest turn in his health to let our friends and family know, when, suddenly, with a kind of audible pop, every overhead light in my house turned on simultaneously—the opposite of a power out-age, a complete power on-age! The overhead light fixture in the living room where I was sitting which I never used, the one in the front sitting room, and the fixture in the kitchen over the table, all went on all at once.

Needless to say, I jumped up, quite startled, rushed through the kitchen to the bedroom where, yes, indeed, that overhead light there, too, was on. And to make things even stranger, when I went to turn it off, I discovered the light switch was already in the "off" position, and yet the light was on. What now? How do you turn a light off that's on when the switch is already off? So, I flipped it on, then off, and thank God, off it went. It already had been a spooky day to start with—the hospice nurse giving me the impression that Paul was about to stop breathing any second—so for me to be sitting on the couch and have every light in my house to turn itself spontaneously on weirded me out even more. I immediately called my night-owl sister on the East Coast to tell her what happened and together we talked me down enough to get a good night's sleep (with all the lights off and staying off).

That night, however, was when a long series of electricity-related happenings began to occur regularly and reliably in tandem with my husband Paul's long, slow transition out of this life. As with the doorbell, I felt impelled to keep a log of these events. A week or so later, at 3 in the morning, out of a sound sleep, I heard my central heating system switch itself on, blowing hot air through the ducts in the bedroom, waking me up. I never turn the heat on at night because I can't sleep if the room is hot, and so the sound of the heat blowing into the bedroom, especially in the dead of night, was unusual, like a freight train coming through. I leapt up, and went out to the living room to look at the thermostat, where once again, as with the lights, the switch for the system was off, but weirdly, the heat was nevertheless on and blowing. So, I stood there for a few moments, half-asleep, trying to figure out how I'm going to turn off the heat when the switch is already off when just as suddenly as it started, I hear the system shut off and the house goes quiet again. The heat did not come on again that night.

A third incident was again in the middle of the night when I turned over only to realize that a bright light was shining in my face. I'm a notoriously fussy sleeper, and I can't sleep with any light shining anywhere. In fact, all of the little lights on the various things I have around—the wireless speakers, the electric toothbrush, the battery chargers—I have them all taped over so I can't see those piercing little lights in the darkness. So, there should have been no reason for anything bright to be shining on my face in the middle of the night. Rousing myself enough to figure it out, I realize that it's the white shower curtain from my adjoining bathroom which is reflecting the light of my living room torchière, as it just so happens, right where my face is lying on the pillow in bed. It's a *very* bright lamp with an extra-strong halogen bulb because I spend a lot of time in the living room reading, which means there was no way I went to bed and forgot to turn it off. And yet, as I stumble out to the living room in the wee hours of the morning, there it was, bright as day, somehow switched on in the middle of the night.

Next, I was taking a nap in the afternoon, between my regular lunch visit to the nursing home and my usual later visit with Paul for dinner, when out of nowhere I heard disco music coming from the other room. Now what? Well, somehow, a very old CD of mine that I had put in the ROM drive of my computer, who knows when or why, had, without any reason, began to play. And of course, all the while all of these electrical incidents are occurring, the doorbell continues to ring randomly without anyone at the door.

Despite the dire prognosis about his imminent demise as pronounced by the hospice nurse in September, Paul did not, after all, rapidly decline and instead the terminal phase of his illness went on for many months, during which time, various lights and appliances in the house would turn themselves on. Both my TV and the VCR went on a couple of times by themselves when the remotes were sitting on a chair across the room, out of my reach. One day, I was enjoying the warm weather of our Bay Area autumn, sitting on the back deck of my house reading when some strange, crackling, staticky noise suddenly erupted from the front room of my house, which I eventually track down to an old battery-operated radio that I had on hand for an emergency. Shoved forgetfully on a bookshelf, the thing just turned itself on again.

One night in December, after Paul had been put to bed and was sleeping soundly, I left the nursing home with a heavy heart. I could feel the end was nearing. My car was parked on the sidewalk right outside where his window to his room was, and I remember that night I was very full of emotion. Understandably, his prolonged decline was taking its toll, and after getting into my car, with the ignition key still in my hand, trying to decide whether or not I needed to cry it out before driving home, all at once, suddenly, every light in the car flashed on at once for about three seconds—the headlights, every notification light on the dashboard, the overhead light, the brake lights, every light in the car—and they all stayed on just long enough for me to be sure that I wasn't imagining it and then, off they went. Stunned, not to say freaked out, this was the first time that any of these electrical phenomena occurred outside of my house. I looked at my hand, somewhat dumbly—yes, the keys were in my hand, they were not in the ignition. And with them still in my hand, I immediately called one of my best friends nearby to tell her about it—I had been keeping her and my sister apprised of all these incidents as they happened—and God bless her, she managed to calm me down enough to get me home.

On telekinesis or paranormal phenomena, I would say, I'm a confirmed agnostic. Many clients and friends have told me of many of their experiences, and I have had no reason to doubt their veracity. It's just that I myself had really not had any similar experiences—until then. And so, even throughout these, I had been trying in the back of my mind this whole time to account for all of the various incidents in my house by speculating on some sort of rational, physical explanation. A random power surge at the house might have triggered the light. Was there a loose circuit on the thermostat? Perhaps I had left the living room lamp on, but the plug was loose and somehow the plug shifted so the light went on. Or maybe the dog stepped on the floor switch.

Stray signals could be tripping the doorbell. Did my computer move from hibernation to active mode and start the CD-ROM drive? And I supposed my sister and my best friend might well have thought what I myself might have thought, had I had a friend or a client telling me about these things: he's a big drama queen, and he's just making this stuff up.

So, in that regard, I was grateful that my sister Carolann was party to witnessing at least one of these strange electrical events with me, during the week she stayed with me following Paul's death and funeral. She and I were sitting in the living room, watching TV, when both of us began to hear something like chanting or singing. So, I mute the TV, we both look at one another, and follow the sound, only to discover that it is my clock radio-CD player in the bedroom which has begun to play the Gregorian chant CD I wake up to every day. The alarm is clearly set for 6 a.m., and yet, it's sometime around 8 p.m. and both of us were sitting in the living room together. As I said, probably like any rational person, my sister could have been forgiven for entertaining a doubt or two everything I had claimed to have gone on. But there we were, both of us, that day, listening to Gregorian chant from a CD player in another room that neither of us had touched.

So, what is the explanation? Is there an explanation? I have no explanation. But after Paul's passing and burial, all of these incidents stopped about as suddenly as they had started. In fact, it has been four years since his death and the doorbell has not rung once by itself again—nor have the lights gone on, nor has the heater started, nor has the computer or radio or CD player begun to play by itself. What was the cause of it all back then? No one really knows. I do not. But here is where I find Jung's notion of synchronicity more useful than any causal explanation because what *is* provable and beyond contesting is how these incidents around my husband's death affected me, what *I* made of them.

First, they were all highly, highly symbolic. One of the great joys of Paul's life had been our house, and of all the aspects of his design, remodeling and creative work on it over the decades, the one he took the most pride in was his learning how to reconfigure and modify the electrical systems. He had been responsible during our relationship for installing all of the light switches, and indeed, he had always been an early adopter of technical hardware and innovations, so the electronic light switch system I have today was indeed the third such system he had installed in our house over the 30 years we owned the place. The emergency radio that crackled static in the middle of the afternoon had originally been Paul's, he had bought it in grad school, and he often mentioned that it was the radio he was listening to when he heard Nixon resign the presidency in 1974. The living room torchière lamp that had gone on in the middle of the night likewise had a bit of familial history: Paul had bought it without consulting me one weekend when I was away on business, a typical practice of his—unilateral shopping— for which I was known to give him a lot of flak. My desktop computer that played the CD was one he had bought and set up for me, and as I thought about it, I realized that the CD player-alarm clock that had gone during my sister's visit had originally been a Christmas gift from him—along with the Gregorian chant CD which was, again, originally his.

As the dust settled after his passing, I then added all of these rich symbolic connections to the original series of electricity-related syn- chronicities—the doorbell—and my perspective shifted a bit further. Was it the bell ringing to herald a visit, albeit immaterial and invisible? And with this idea my sense of the weird and frightening at the time suddenly mellowed and all of what had happened began to feel as if Paul, having needed to leave his beloved home due to his illness and destined, sadly, never to return home, was nevertheless still very vividly, energetically, brightly, still with me, very much there.

The paranormal "explanations" for these events—indeed all such events—are impossible not to imagine. And we can certainly go there. Was his spiritual life-energy gradually freed from the confines of his material body so that, though still alive at the nursing home, his spirit was nevertheless able in some willful way to signal his deep desire to stay in his house by turning these things on? Was it a stubborn refusal on his part to let the darkness and extinction of death take him by turning things on, still, as long as he could? One thing people who knew Paul well—his family and me—could definitely attest to was his stubbornness and his need to control his external environment.

Or was it not him at all but me? Was it my own unconscious energy being loosed around me as our material relationship in this life was coming to an end? Was it my own need for illumination being manifested in ways that felt uncanny and ego-alien and yet came from levels of my own psyche? It's natural and normal in our cause-and-effect habit of thought to spin out conjecture as to what the occult causes of such telekinetic events might be. Who knows? Maybe our life energy, as it is freed from our bodies, does indeed manifest in distinct ways in the material world around us through a process we do not yet have the capacity to empirically prove. There are plenty of such stories about the palpable force of the soul's energy leaving the body at the moment of death across culture and time.

Absent anything other than conjecture, though, what we are left with beyond such speculations is Jung's insight into our own psychological, emotional and symbolic experience, and for me, in sum, during that difficult and long transition of his between life and death, the one thing I did not feel was alone. I was being visited; the doorbell was ringing. Nor was I in the dark; literally, the lights were on. Nor was I left in silence; again, literally, the music was playing. In this most momentous of transitions in my life, the loss of my husband, I was given a long series of synchronicities which accompanied me, between light and dark, between sound and silence, and in the end, between my life and his death.

Phenomena around the time of a family member's death often have synchronistic resonances, as with my story here and Jung's story from his autobiography much earlier in this book, but, as we have seen with meeting our soul mates or sharing our lives with siblings, sometimes the actual, literal time of a loved one's death is the synchronistic element. The particular form of synchronicity has happened to me personally twice and both in conjunction with friends of mine from my church. The first I found out about when returning from my time back in New Jersey after the death of my mother on March 29, 2001, specifically, I learned from my friend Carol from my faith sharing group at church that she herself had just returned from Boston and her father's funeral after his death on the same day, March 29, 2001. Both of us were struck by the coincidence of the dates, and it's been a point of contact between the two of us ever since, knowing that both our parents were, as we Catholics say, "born into eternal life" on the same day. As Carol has sometimes said, and I agree, it makes their absence a little easier, knowing that in a way, symbolically, by the coincidence of the dates, they were together in their passage.

The second, similar coincidence also was friends of mine from church, Dave and Patrick, a lovely older male couple who I had gotten to know through our Peace and Social Justice committee that I had organized and run for some time. Dave had been a priest but had left the ministry quite some time ago when he met Patrick, and the two of them, by the time I met them, had been together many years. Warm, wonderful guys, a little bit older than myself, but given the regularity of seeing them together every Sunday at Mass together, along with our participation on our social justice group and other parish events outside of Mass, they became over the years part of what I would call my church family.

It was a stunning thing then that Sunday when, not seeing them there in the pew, I instead heard Patrick's name read aloud during our prayers of the faithful, asking for the repose of his soul. Patrick had died?! Hearing of the passing of a fellow parishioner during the prayers is definitely never the best way of being informed, but in a large urban parish and at a time before social networking was what it is now in our lives, that often was the case. Immediately after Mass, I went to some friends and yes, indeed, they told me it was true, Patrick had died that week, and from what Dave told them, it came out of the blue. The two of them were watching TV on the couch, and in literally a minute, Patrick collapsed and was gone before Dave could even call emergency services, the cause as yet undetermined, but likely a massive heart attack or stroke. The date: April 29, 2005. A heavy cloud hung over my thoughts that week until the funeral Mass the following Saturday, which was the first time I got to speak with Dave in person, who, despite it all, was holding up fairly well.

Nevertheless, understandably, it was a huge loss to him and for all of us in the parish, and in the months that followed, when I'd come into the church and see Dave, by himself, in the pew, it didn't seem right. They had been together so long, and like so many long-term couples, they seem to "belong" together. For that reason, more than one Sunday morning for Mass, I sat with him, and as the time passed, the pain of grief grew less little by little. But it was also clear, not just from Dave's appearance, but as he eventually told me explicitly, that his own health was not good. He had been diagnosed since Patrick's death with cancer and was doing all he could to fight it, but was I wrong to spy underneath his brave face a level of resignation and acceptance? I'll never know.

So, as the year passed, Dave declined, and I along with his other friends in the parish prepared myself for the inevitable news. Our congregation, I suppose, like many in these latter days, has a high proportion of older parishioners, so the passing of these members of my church family are part of the regular cycle of life, sad but not usually shocking, and the news of their deaths is always an opportunity for us the living to reflect on the mysteries of what lies beyond and to call upon their spiritual presence as we go about our sacred rituals. Eventually Dave became so sick that he was no longer able to attend Sunday morning Mass. So, when I didn't see Dave in the pew, I didn't initially think much about it, and took my usual place on the side. But that's when a friend of mine came up to me and told me that Friday morning, there would be a funeral mass and interment for Dave, for he had passed away that week.

Though we Catholics don't have a specific tradition like the *yahrzeit* in Judaism of honoring the anniversary of a loved one's death, because of my interest in coincidences, as well as my own internal emotional time clock, something nagged at me throughout Mass, and I knew that Dave's partner Patrick had died just last year around this time, sometime right after Easter. I discovered afterward that I was right. Intuition is fine, but facts are facts, and using the online obituaries I discovered that it wasn't just around the same time Patrick had died but that in fact, Dave had died *on the very same day* as Patrick, exactly one year later, April 29, 2006. Certainly a coincidence, and a meaningful one, at least to me, and I speculate, in some way, to them as well. Was Dave thinking about Patrick who had the year before passed out of his own life on that day, April 29, as Dave came to the end of his own earthly life? Having known their devotion to one another over so many years, to know their lives concluded together through this oddly apt identity of dates helped those of us who knew and loved them imagine that as in life, so in death, they were together.

A more extended story from my friend Lorie has all the elements I've been discussing about the relationship of synchronistic events and the death of our loved ones—preparatory synchronicities and syn-chronicities of times and dates—but it introduces yet another one that I've come across in hearing these stories: the way in which a synchronistic event can sometimes act in a consolatory way, helping us toward an acceptance of the loss and moving us back into the new and changed life now before us without them.

Lorie sat down one day with me over a cup of coffee on the bench near my office to recount the long and varied series of synchronistic events that preceded her husband Allen's eventual passing from kidney cancer at a relatively young age. These events, she said, didn't even at the time feel to her like random coincidences but, as with my own experiences above, she said she felt that she and her husband were being readied to face the rapid and very unexpected loss each of them were to encounter.

"As I prepared myself to talk with you today," she said to me, "I began to think, the way you do, about where I would start the story, and if I tell the truth, really, the synchronistic events around Allen's death actually began long before he died. So, in a way it's a bit like a puzzle, where the most vivid pieces sort of naturally fit together right away and you go, 'uh huh, sure!' Looking back, however, you realize there actually were other pieces that were also parts of the puzzle, pieces of the experience of his death that came in advance and that, I believe, allowed me—maybe even prepared me—to face what he and I would have to face together later.

"For example, in December, 2011, my family booked a flight to visit my father and mother, because my father at that time was dying of kidney cancer. So there we all are, my family, all set to go, when just before we all are about to leave, two days before, suddenly my husband—who had never suffered from kidney stones before—had to be rushed to hospital in tremendous pain with what was described to us, after a bunch of tests, as a probable kidney stone. Now this was an extraordinarily inconvenient circumstance, both time-wise and, of course, for Allen who was in extreme pain. But in the end, a kidney stone is nothing at all life-threatening. So his doctor told the rest of us that we all might as well continue on with our travel plans to visit my parents. The plan at that point was to use keyhole surgery to remove Allen's stone, which was relatively large from what they could see. Because of that, the outcome of other options for its removal were less certain and probably would be equally, if not, more painful. The good news was, if all went as planned, my husband would be in fine shape to join us after a few days, so we did as the doctor said, and with a sense of relief, we changed his outbound flight, and off we all went, without him."

Lorie paused here, took a sip of her coffee and looked at me a bit sadly. "In the end, however, none of that happened. A subsequent series of tests cast doubt on whether it was a kidney stone after all, so the surgery never took place, and doctor after doctor was really unable to tell us anything. And of course, this is all happening long-distance— Allen there and the rest of the family in New York. So, after three weeks of this medical folderol, Allen himself decided he'd had enough, checked himself out of the hospital and made the trip over to New York to join us. Which was when, just seven days later, all hell broke loose medically. Intense, unbearable pain, blood, you name it, at which point Allen was rushed to the hospital in Bridgeport, Connecticut, which is, incidentally, and I would say, significantly, the town where I was born. And that was where, suddenly, with no more warning than that, Allen died.

"Only afterward, to our enormous shock, did we find out that Allen had had an undiagnosed kidney tumor—in fact, the identical kind of cancer my father had had and was dying of, which, you remember, was the very reason for our visit back to my parents in the first place. In Allen's case, however, the tumor had burst, which had been the cause of the pain that he'd experienced some weeks earlier. Once burst, we found out in retrospect, there was no coming back. Now, in the large scope of things, kidney cancer is pretty rare and of course my husband and my father weren't related. So, the weird synchronicity of my fifty-year old husband dying in the very town where I was born, passing away unexpectedly 10 days before my father, and from the same condition that had occasioned our visit back there is a network of coincidences the meaning of which I still ponder to this day. If you wrote it in a novel, people would accuse you of too much creative license, but that is what happened. And yet, as I have pondered on all of it over these interceding years, I've found that other somewhat meaningful coincidences about his death came to my mind, all of which has led me to think about the fabric of our life together and how on some deep level what was to be my unexpected loss of him had already begun much, much earlier to tug at the connection between us.

"So, another story.... About a year and a half or maybe even two years before my husband died, I had a dream, the details of which I don't actually remember, but when I woke up, its impact left me terrified specifically around the fact neither of us had life insurance. I'll be the first to admit, that might seem a somewhat quirky and overly specific concern, and yet, in my defense, I'm sure I'm not really the first person in the world to wake up in the middle of the night and per-severate about money and security. Back then, we weren't particularly poor or rich, my husband was healthy, and we had some savings but, out of nowhere precisely because of this dream, I found myself sweating bullets about our long-term financial prospects, even though we'd been without life insurance for a number of years."

Lorie laughed a little. "I'm sure Allen thought me a bit mad when I woke him up that night to tell him he had to get life insurance right away—obviously that was not something we were going to be doing at 3 a.m., even if in our instantaneous internet age where we probably could get life insurance immediately in the middle of the night from somewhere—but from that point forward, every once in a while, I would remind him we needed to get life insurance. Now, I will say, I wasn't neurotic or frantic about it, but the effect of the dream stuck and I was convinced that it was a prudent step to take, so my asking him to get the life insurance situation sorted out became a regular thing between us. Nevertheless, he delayed and, I suppose like many people when it comes to issues of their own mortality, he seemed he didn't want to face it, so time just kept going by until, finally one day, Allen found out we could sign up for life insurance through our bank, which is what we eventually did.

"Interestingly enough, about the same time we did that, it was my husband's turn to have a dream, and in his dream, he discovered that he had bought a winning lottery ticket at a store in our hometown, and when he came out of the store after finding this out, he looked up in the sky and noticed a church steeple. Allen was so impressed by how vivid this dream was—and maybe a little hopeful that it would come true—such that he drove all around our town trying to find a store like the one in his dream which sold lottery tickets within view of a church steeple. After some wandering and searching, he did actually identify such a store close to a church, though he had to admit the view of the steeple was not the same as the one he had dreamt: in the dream, the steeple was very pronounced and it had a big cross on top of it. Still— you can't win if you don't play—he bought at least some of his weekly lottery tickets there, for quite some time after.

"Fast forward to the time immediately after his death, and that was when, quite uncannily, it struck me about the two dreams we'd each had—my dream of life insurance and his dream of winning the lottery. Of course, they were both weirdly, almost clairvoyantly connected. Why? Because, after Allen's death, when talking to the life insurance company, I was informed that the benefit would in the end be paid out to me, since the policy had, quite fortuitously, been in force for a full 14 months, whereas, had we delayed much longer so that the policy had been in force for only 12 months or less—standard policy for life insurance companies to prevent fraud or abuse—the company would *not* have paid out the death benefit And when I heard that news from the agent, I immediately thought of *Allen's* dream, and said to myself,

'Oh my God. Allen did win the lottery all right, only I'm the one collecting the prize money.'

"I know that sounds crass to say out loud, but in order to understand it, you'd have to know more about my husband's psychology. Allen was fifty years old when he died and so healthy he wasn't even registered with a doctor. That's the lottery part of the story— the sheer chance that someone in seemingly perfect health would die so quickly of a completely rare and undiagnosed cancer, leaving life insurance, only purchased frankly in the nick of time, and though not a large policy, it was still what my husband would have called 'life changing money.' And it was. That money made all the difference for me and my children in the chaotic period after his and my father's death.

"But the lottery image also struck me later, after all this happened, as having perhaps a somewhat darker meaning. Was the dream saying in the broadest possible way to my husband in a way we couldn't have imagined at the time, 'your number is up'? Of course, he didn't see it like that at all. nor did I, nor could we have ever thought that the lottery at play was in fact the very wheel of his life and that money we would be coming into, 'winning,' would actually be won through a tremendous and awful loss.

"But even that is not yet the end of the synchronicities, for the intersecting connections of our respective dreams made me consider even more deeply the events of the year before he died, that last year of his life of which we were so blissfully unaware of being his last. Then I remembered something else that had happened. One day, during a period of time when he and I had been going through a rough time with one another, I took the situation between us to prayer, and as sometimes happens to me, I was given a word of knowledge, one for myself and one for my husband. My word was, 'Take off his grave clothes and let him go,' from the story of Lazarus in the Gospel of John,

Jesus' telling Lazarus's grieving sisters Mary and Martha to unbind their brother from his grave clothes so that he can be raised from the dead.

"And the word that came to me for my husband was, in fact, the very next line in the gospel story, "Lazarus, come out!" Jesus' command to his dead friend to rise out of the grave where he had been laid and to resume his life. In one way, I guess, it made some sense that these words of knowledge came together for me and my husband, because after all the two verses are practically next to each other in the bible, so that didn't feel especially noteworthy. I did wonder if I was wrong in the way, intuitively, I had separated the two verses into which was for him and which was for me—was I making that up? In any case, I just went with it, taking the time to write out the words I felt were meant for him on a piece of paper and, as part of working things out between us, I gave the note to him.

"So, about a month after he died, I went to a church service, and wouldn't it so happen that in fact the Gospel passage for that Sunday was the very story of Lazarus. Speechless, with my heart was in my throat, I heard the story being read, and I knew—just *knew*—God was talking to me. I remained as composed as I could, and the preacher said quite a few things I no longer remember. One thing he did say which I do recall vividly was that this story of Lazarus, included in the gospel to foreshadow Christ's own resurrection from the dead, was to show us that death could be both an ending and a beginning, depending on how you interpreted the symbol of the tomb and the nature of life. Yes, Lazarus raised by Jesus was coming out of the tomb to return to the earth and his former life, but it could also be said that coming out of the tomb could also symbolize being awakened to the inevitable reality of death and the eternal life our soul enjoys beyond the grave. In all my years of church, I had never heard that passage discussed in that way.

"Which then suddenly, retrospectively, made sense of a synchronistic event I hadn't fully understood on the very day of my husband's funeral. I was in the bedroom, getting ready, when a book fell off the highest shelf and with some force. I was nowhere near the bookcase, and so, I figured it was my husband who had knocked it off the shelf. As I said, this was the day of his funeral. Picking it up, I saw that it was one of those really offbeat spiritual books that belonged to him, a book I'd never seen before. I read English perfectly well, but the book was very hard to understand, except for one passage on the very page I had opened up where—though this book was not at all Christian—Jesus was saying, 'Everyone is focused on the nature of my death, the violence and the blood.' This particular image caught me up short, for, remember now, my husband died of internal bleeding caused by the ruptured tumor. And in this book that fell off the shelf that I'm reading just hours before Allen's funeral, Jesus goes then to say, "it was a violent and shocking death but people forget that for most of my life I was, as I am now, alive.'

"So there I was, the morning of Allen's funeral, reading a passage that reminded of the life we live beyond this life in Jesus' own words, not just in the book that fell off the shelf, but also in the story of Lazarus which appeared to me in prayer before his death. There is no proof to this, naturally, but in my heart, I feel these words came to me, both before and after his death, to remind me of his continued presence in my life even today. He is dead and yet he continues to live."

The story of Lorie's experiences around her husband's death are moving for anyone who has had to survive the sudden and unantici-pated loss of a loved one, but as synchronistic experiences, I feel they are also instructive to us. I might say that when the ordinary reader of a book like this thinks of what does or doesn't make a coincidence synchronistic, he or she probably has in mind the kind of events that had occurred to me: dramatic, bordering on the paranormal, with immediate impact that one cannot ignore.

Lorie's more extended narrative illustrates many aspects of meaningful coincidences at the time of a loved one's passing. Certainly, extraordinarily synchronistic was the strange intersection of the nature of her father's and her husband's respective illnesses and deaths—both passing from the same rare illness within days of one another, and after a set of circumstances which, without any conscious intention on Lorie's part, had brought her back to her own hometown. Redolent of T. S. Eliot's classic lines from "Little Gidding" in *Four Quartets,* "...and the end of all our exploring will be to arrive where we started and know the place for the first time," (T. S. Eliot, "Little Gidding," *Four Quartets.* New York: Mariner Books, 1968), Lorie finds herself in the place where her life started—her hometown—to face the end of her father's life as well as the end of her husband's—but she finds herself there not on purpose, and instead by pure chance.

I am inclined to call this sort of meaningful coincidence a "classic" synchronicity, because its significance is indeed immediate and undeniable to the person experiencing it at the very time it happens. Lorie's, moreover, very much exemplifies the special quality that family synchronicities manifest in our lives, bringing our attention to the dense network of connection that is our family for us in our lives: beginning and ending so close together, husband and father taken so soon and in the exact same way. One doesn't need to search for significance with such a "classic" synchronicity. It is simply there.

The other series of events Lorie told me about concerning her husband's passing are just as synchronistic, of course, but in a slightly different way, and they disclose a different but no less important and valid aspect of Jung's thoughts on the notion. These I am tempted to call "revealed" synchronicities: not evident or meaningful at the time they occurred but, only in the course of subsequent events does their significance become clear, profound, and undeniable. When Lorie had her dream of the life insurance or when the Bible verses came to her in prayer, though each of these events certainly had an impact on her, as she described it, but neither was at the time yet synchronistic. It was only after Allen's death that the earlier experiences they had "coincided," fit together, completed, illuminated the subsequent situations to produce for her that "aha" experience of making a meaningful connection that is the essence of synchronicity.

It is this sort of "revealed" synchronicity that had led skeptics at my lectures or among my readership (even some of my editors!) to criticize Jung's idea of synchronicity or, if not his idea, then my own take on the topic, for it was only Lorie's subsequent reflection upon the connections between the previous and later events that ended up "making" them meaningful to her. In other words, the dream of life insurance and the subsequent fortuitousness of its timing, or Allen's dream of the lottery and its imagery, the full symbolic import of which was only disclosed later after he had died, are meanings which Lori herself "made up" afterwards, in retrospect. Synchronicity, therefore, say the naysayers, is actually not a real thing. It's something we all "make up," by looking at patterns and connections after the fact.

To which I say: exactly! Indeed, I would argue, that *is* Jung's very idea and, far from mistaken, it is precisely what he wanted to convey by coining the concept synchronicity. Jung was not a physicist. He was a psychiatrist. His interest was in validating the interior world of our own subjective experience, and he knew from his work as a clinician, that our psychological healing comes from—indeed, can *only* come from—our ability to make meaning of our lives. Yes, the meaning of our lives is *made*, not just given, and it is made from the principle of our capacity to make connections and experience wholeness. I some-times say, rather cheekily, that the meaning of our lives is something we go out and find lying under a rock. We are agents, active agents, of our own significance. We *make* our lives meaningful, and we do so in the way that I did or that Lorie did—by actively taking the events of our lives, reflecting on their impact and connection, and finding in them the significance that makes sense of what we have lived.

However, given the theme of this book, I'd like to say virtually the same thing about our families, also well-exemplified by Lorie's stories about Allen's transition out of this life. Her reflections after Allen's passing knit together parts of her inner experience with subsequent outer events until, in the end, the connections she made had the effect of grounding her in the fabric of her family, the family she came from and the family she had created through her relationship with her husband. The synchronistic events around his death showed her how she was connected. In fact, the very temporal discontinuity of them—that they did *not* occur, as some synchronistic events do, in close temporal proximity—but rather had the character of being stretched, as it were, across time and space in her life, was deeply symbolic, *is* deeply symbolic of how we exist in our families. Our family connections are not just for now—they extended back into the past and into the future, past death—and they are only as significant as we make them for ourselves.

As I have said, people often complain to me that synchronistic events never occur to them. They hear me talk and tell these stories, or they read these books, and they long for this kind of dramatic occurrence in their lives, something that will just "happen" that will deliver a meaningful life onto the doorstep of their experience. What I think such individuals miss—and which I try with both my clients and others to put as tactfully as I might—is the above point: that meaning comes about through the connections we ourselves make. By allowing ourselves to reflect and see, as Lorie did, how we are connected to those we love, that is where the meaning of families is to be *found*, not uncovered "out there" but *fashioned*, of the events we live day to day with our families.

Sometimes synchronicities precede, prepare, even perhaps predict the death of a loved one. That was certainly my case and the same with Lori. But by the same token, as aspects of our unconscious capacity for wholeness, meaningful coincidences can also console and repair the dis-integration we live when we lose a family member. Sometimes these events serve to remind us, in the midst of our grief, that the physical connection that has been taken away is only the material dimension of the relationship, but that actually, in a larger way, that attachment, that love, nevertheless continues for us *im*-materially, that is to say, both spiritually and psychologically for us the living. As with all synchronistic events, we have seen that what I have come to call these "consolatory synchronicities" may range from dramatic to subtle, but when they happen to us, they serve to restore that continuity of connection which our family always represents for us, the bond of love that transcends time and physical death.

My long-time colleague from Pacifica Graduate Institute in Santa Barbara, Robyn was gracious enough to tell her story to me about the loss of her sister and how a synchronistic event in her life played a part in completing the circle.

"It was only in May 2012 that I found out that my sister Maralee, my best friend my entire life, had passed away the year before, most likely due to complications from early-onset dementia. It's a long and complicated family story, and I could go into some detail, but suffice it to say my brother is not a nice person and had secluded my sister from any outside contact for the last couple of years of her life. At the time I found out she was gone, I had not seen her in four years; the longest period I had gone without contact with her in my life. And the synchronicity starts there….

"Were this story somewhere other than a book, I would have liked to attach the video that I created after I found out about Maralee's passing, which was only due to a chance synchronistic event itself, since it was not my brother or any other relative that told me. Rather, I received an alert from Ancestry.com via email that there was a possible "leaf"—that is to say, an additional entry—on my family tree. When I went on the site to look, indeed, it was my sister's obituary with her name spelled incorrectly.

"I think you can understand when I found out that my favorite person in the world had passed away—not to mention the way I found out that I had lost my sister—I needed to *do…something*. Luckily, I am the keeper of our family's boxes and boxes of old photos. So that was when I began to create the video of Maralee using scanned photos. The hours and hours of work it took to organize, scan, and edit was a good thing, a healing thing, and kept my mind off the reality of the loss. It was then that I felt moved to take the next step forward, and I began to plan a memorial service for Maralee here on the campus where I work. It would be held in the Sacred Circle, near our newly built grotto. Maralee had also worked at Pacifica with me for many years, about seven or eight, I believe, and she loved this place like I do; the grounds, the butterflies, the bunnies, the beautiful landscape, and the sacred secrets that are held here. In fact, that's another very synchronistic element of not just her passing but of our relationship throughout our lives. We had actually worked many years together, starting together in the 70s in Los Angeles at the advertising firm of Chiat/Day, and through a very unintentional series of circumstances, we both ended up at Pacifica together in the 2000s. I knew she would have loved the memorial service I was planning on campus for her and her former colleagues and friends.

"Now, going back a few years, it turns out while Maralee was working at Pacifica, she was called to jury duty in Ventura, showing up each day for the whole week to see if she was called to serve on a jury. She never was, but during those days, she and another woman also called for jury duty ended up becoming friends with one another, chatting, eating lunch together, that sort of thing, and in the course of their getting to know one another, Maralee shared her work stories about the school with this woman, who was very interested in the school. In fact, after their jury service had ended, this woman stayed in close touch with Maralee, inquired about Pacifica and the programs offered, and in the end was so impressed that she applied to the Mythological Studies program, was accepted, completed her course-work and her dissertation, earning her doctorate from Pacifica. So, naturally, when I began planning the memorial for Maralee at Pacifica,

I tried hard to remember this woman's name. I knew she would have wanted to be at the service; to share in this grieving process. However, for the life of me, I could not remember her name. Of course, I worked at Pacifica so you would think that my scouring through years of Mythological Studies student rosters trying to find a name would jog my memory, but I could not find or remember anything. I went to our receptionist, Jeannette, who has worked here a very long time too. Jeannette remembered the stories and could almost "see" this woman, but she could not remember her name either. I eventually stopped trying to figure out who this woman was and simply proceeded to plan the memorial to be held one year after my sister's passing, on June 16, 2012.

"Now, sometime during the beginning of 2012, I began conversations with a woman named Janet who was an editor. We wanted to add her to our "outside editor list" that we provide to students who may need some extra help in their writing process. Janet was familiar with Pacifica and the particular style we use here at the school for the students' work—she herself had graduated from Pacifica in 2009, and I remember loving her dissertation topic—plus she had a special interest in wanting to work with students in the area of Mythological Studies. After vetting her qualifications, I was happy to add her name. About two months after Janet was added to our "outside editor" list, the department decided to create a position for an in-house proofreader to serve exclusively with those Myth students. I asked this newer person, Janet, if she would like to switch over to that position. All dissertation students are required to work with the school's in-house editor for the final review of their work prior to publishing. Lucky for us, she agreed! That was how we began our wonderful working relationship in early 2012. I quickly bonded with Janet, and we became fast friends.

"However, it was in early 2013—that is, six months after my sister's memorial service and almost a year after beginning a professional relationship and personal friendship with Janet that I received an email from her, saying 'It was me!' At first, I had no idea what she was talking about and thought I had missed another email or voicemail from her. I was not working in the office at the time, out on medical leave after having rotator cuff surgery. I hadn't been on campus in quite some time; I was still recovering at home. While I was out, just by chance, Janet had decided to drop by campus and say hello to some people, and also participate in a class with the Myth Program, which was when our receptionist, Jeannette, took one look at her and remembered who she was.

"Janet was the woman my sister sat with in jury duty, became friends with, and who subsequently went to, and graduated from, Pacifica. Janet—the woman with whom I had now become friends—was *the woman my sister had befriended during jury duty. Janet.*

"Naturally, I got back to her immediately, and caught her up on all that had happened with Maralee, her passing, the video, the memorial service, the time I had spent trying to find her so she could attend the service and how much she had meant to Maralee and now to me. We spent quite a while that day crying with each other. But, in the end, I still have a hard time believing how it all played out. Maralee became Janet's friend, and as Janet now says, Maralee guided her to me to become friends after she was gone from this earthly plane. So, although I have probably hundreds of synchronicity stories in my life—seriously they happen all the time to me—this one is by far my favorite and the one most dear to my heart."

Another such consolatory synchronicity comes from a dear friend whom I shall call Anthony. Suicide is an issue that has had a deep effect on my life, both as a psychotherapist who must contend regularly with my clients' thoughts, feelings and occasionally, unfortunately, attempts to kill themselves, but also personally. I, myself, am a survivor of suicide in my family—my father's father committed suicide four years before I born and my brother-in-law likewise, during the early years of my relationships with Paul. So, I have now participated twice in an event held in San Francisco, called The Overnight, which raises money for the American Foundation for Suicide Prevention, a 20-mile overnight walk that starts at sundown and ends at sunrise, as a symbol of walking through the night of surviving the suicide of a loved one. As part of my fundraising efforts, I ask those who contribute to my walk if they would like me to memorialize someone in their lives whom they have lost to suicide, pledging to write their name on a ribbon and wear it on my T-shirt during my walk. The first time I did the walk, I was very surprised to hear from people I had known for many, many years who had never talked about the person in their life they had lost in this fashion. I thought I had known all there was to know about them. But no, there is still a stigma and a shame about this manner of death. That first walk I ended up with no less than 44 names pinned to my T-shirt, fluttering in the warm summer evening of my pilgrimage throughout the city to honor the dead and prevent further acts of self-harm. It was during preparations for my second walk, as I was also gathering stories for this present book, that my friend Anthony told me about a con-solatory synchronicity which occurred to him in the course of his brother's death by suicide.

"Carl had always been very troubled," Anthony said to me, "and troubled in a wide variety of ways that defied all of my parents' best intentions. Looking back, I think it's clear he had a number of different kinds of learning disabilities from the start of schooling. Back then, however, there wasn't a very sophisticated understanding of those things, and so, right from the beginning, many of his difficulties were labeled as behavioral problems and treated as disciplinary matters, rather than as manifestations of his need for help. By the time it became clear that discipline wasn't what was really needed, and that perhaps psychiatric help was in order, I think the devastation to his self-esteem was such that maybe no amount of counseling or medication might have helped. But even then the doctors couldn't really decide what the right diagnosis or treatment was. Was he schizophrenic? Clinically depressed? Manic depressive? I heard all those terms thrown about as a kid growing up in the shadow of Carl. And as he got older, he fell into a particular social crowd and began to do what we now call self-medicating, you know, drinking and using drugs pretty regularly to deal with his pain and his issues. The whole situation was super hard on the family—my parents most of all—and I think by the time he had barely graduated high school, they more or less realized that there was very little they were going to be able to do to help him or save him from himself.

"In a way, he was a cautionary example for me. I was a somewhat quiet kid, and watching all this drama when I was growing up made me pretty much who I am today, that is, someone who likes order and consistency, not a big risk-taker. But Carl was totally the opposite. During my teenage years, he was coming and going, usually showing up when he needed something, often stealing things from my parents to finance his drug use, which was very upsetting. He even stole stuff from me now and then, little electronics, pieces of jewelry. That eventually stopped after a few years, and I realized that that was because I heard through the grapevine that instead of just using, he was now dealing drugs and had gotten hooked up, through one of his stays in the county jail, with a crew of folks that were known in our neighborhood for doing that sort of thing. So that's now where he was making a living.

"All of us who knew him, all of my family, knew that none of this was going to end well for Carl. We had plenty of examples of this kind of stuff in our neighborhood—guys on the streets, using, dealing—and they all came to a bad end. So, when I was 23, I got the call from my dad, the call we had all been expecting. Carl was gone. But not just gone. As my father said, and I'll never forget it, 'Your brother killed himself today.' As the details came out through the police, Carl had jumped from a roof in the middle of a drug run. It's one thing to expect the worst, but it's another thing when you get news of it. I remember the silence on the phone that day between my dad and me. It seemed like forever. Very, very painful. Neither of my parents were up to going and identifying him. So, along with my girlfriend at the time, I did that task. And it was just as well that I did, because it was a brutal business. Given the condition of his body, the identification was made simply on the basis of some tattoos on his arms and legs that I knew he had. I didn't actually see him, because he really wasn't in a fit condition to be seen, and it fell on me largely to make all the arrangements. To this day, I can say, I don't think my parents have ever recovered from it all. They've experienced so much guilt and shame, what could they have done better or differently, was there any way to have saved him? I personally have made my peace with it, but that was because of what I'm going to tell you.

"So, Carl had an apartment, and I'm thinking maybe a week or two after he killed himself, it occurs to me that I should probably go over and see what's there, talk to the landlord, you know, wind things up. The landlord knew what had happened, so he lets me in and he tells me he's going to get rid of Carl's stuff if that's OK with me, to vacate the place for another tenant. The place was more or less a dump, not just his apartment but the whole complex, in a bad part of town, kind of slummy, and once I'm in the apartment, it's exactly what you'd expect from a drug user—virtually no furniture, there's a bed and chair, fridge has some beer and like, ketchup packages from take-out food. There's nothing really to get rid of. So, I go into the bedroom and check out the closet and Carl's got some clothes in there, you know, shirts, jeans, nothing special, but he does have this once-upon-a-time nice black leather jacket that he got a long time ago and evidently hung on to. The place reeks of dope, and I remember thinking that I'd like the jacket, as a way to remember him, and because it's a nice jacket, but the thing would need to aired out for a month till it stopped smelling like marijuana. Anyway, I leave, tell the landlord he's doing us a favor by getting rid of Carl's stuff, feel free, and that day, I take the jacket, and the thing is literally stinking up my car as I go to the dry cleaners where I'm going to just hand it over to them to see what they can do.

"At the cleaners, before I give it to them, I'm going through the pockets when I come upon a bunch of papers, and it looks like Carl's writing, but I don't look at them right away. When I go back to the car, I unfold them and start reading. At first, I was a little freaked out because I was afraid it was a suicide note, because he was writing things about wanting to die, wanting the pain to end, feeling hopeless, but it's clear that he wrote this all out at some point when he was high on...whatever. Maybe recently, maybe not, I couldn't tell, but it looked pretty recent to me. However, then, I come across a piece of paper—these are all written on a little yellow lined note pad—which looks more coherent, and it starts 'to my loved ones' and then goes on, essentially, to address us— my parents and me, his girlfriend, some of his childhood friends. And he says very simply, 'what will be will be. I've done my best to escape all of it. No one is responsible. What happens to me does not mean anything. I love you all.' In other words, a statement of love for us and, the way I would put it, a release of any responsibility we might feel for the outcome of his life. Easier said than done or felt, sure, but it was the one thing after his death that I think about even today which made it bearable at least for me. I shared it with my parents, naturally, but there was so much water under the bridge at that point, they just dismissed it as a crazy note and continue to feel the burden of guilt.

"But for me, it made a big difference. It was written, from what I could tell, in a moment of clarity, and I do believe he meant what he said; he did love us, he did try his best, and he did accept what was going to happen to him. And I also get shivers a little when I think about what if—what if I hadn't gone over there, what if I hadn't gone through that jacket. That's the element of chance in the story. I really would have, even today, a whole different attitude toward my brother and toward how he died, if I hadn't found that note. But I did. And it's helped me accept what happened."

Of all the stories I have heard in my 25 years of research and writing on the nature of synchronicity, the story of Charlotte and what happened to her after the death of her son Todd still sticks in my mind, even though she told me her story over 20 years ago. Todd was a college student at the time of his death, a very big personality, as she described him to me—an athlete and a scholar, never could sit still, very social. Some of this energy she was describing you could really see in the various pictures she showed me of him when we talked: the big smile, the very direct gaze into the camera, the kind of young man who really looked ready to take his life in his hands and run with it. He was at school at the time, rounding the corner to the last semester of his senior year, and had just been home for Christmas break. He and his circle had had a New Year's Eve party planned at a friend's house near campus. So, on the morning of December 31, off he went on the five-hour drive back to school in southern California.

Tragically, he never made it. That afternoon, a drunk driver swerved into the oncoming lane of traffic on a small two-lane road, totaling Todd's car and killing him instantly, and because of the extensive damage done to his body in the course of the accident, Charlotte and her husband were advised by the medical examiners that it was likely better for them to forego a physical identification of the body. They took this advice, then held a closed-casket funeral for Todd, and an eventual cremation.

"All of it was unimaginably hard," she told me, "but I must say, not being able to see him one last time was the part of it that, for me at least, was hardest of all. It's such a visceral bond you have with your child, especially for a mother. You share your body for nine months with him, he looks like you and your husband, you spend so much time taking care of him for so many years, making sure he's safe, healthy, fed. Because of how he was killed, not being able to see Todd and have at least that small bit of physical, literal closure was just devastating for me. And it stayed that way for me for months afterward. At the time, I really could not have done anything else, however, I was tormented by the fact that I would never see him again.

In fact, as time passed, it didn't get better. If anything, I felt worse and worse—about not having had a chance to say goodbye, about not having been, in my mind, courageous enough to face what had happened, about not demanding as the person that brought him into this world that I see him in whatever state. My husband kept telling me that I had—we had—done the right thing, that it was better for me to remember him the way he had been, and not have my last image of my son be something grisly or horrible. But having listened to everyone else about what was best, the result was that I was left feeling profoundly bereft. Not actually *seeing* him seemed to be what I started, in my grief, to get in a way fixated upon, so I would sit sometimes and just go over and over the photo albums, looking at all the pictures we had taken, thinking to myself, 'No more, Charlotte. No more. Todd's gone. No more memories.' And over time it began to wear on both of us, my inability to go on. You hear that, how people's marriages break up after the death of a child, but until it happens to you, you can't imagine. But now, talking about this years after, I see how I was just stuck in my grief and that I had become quite an emotional burden on my husband who, of course, was also struggling massively under his own grief about Todd.

"So, one day in the middle of the aftermath of it, I am sitting at home crying over the photo albums, and I mean that literally: I am sitting with the albums in my lap, at whatever time it was, 2:15 p.m., 3 o'clock, crying and repeating to myself what had become this awful mantra at the time, 'If I could only see him one more time, if only I could see him one more time,' when I hear the mailman come. So, I put aside the photo albums and there, unbelievably, is a big manila envelope from Todd. All the hair on my head stood up, and I was covered in chills. The envelope was pretty beat up and when I looked at it, I saw that it had been mailed the day Todd was killed, December 31. At first, this didn't make a whole lot of sense to my poor confused mind, and I briefly thought someone was pulling a terrible prank on me. But then I looked and sure enough, it was Todd's writing, he had written our names on the envelope himself. When I opened it up, there was a handwritten note from him, along with a whole bunch of pictures of him and of all of us from that last Christmas together. He must have had them developed at some one-hour photo developing place on his way back to school, without our knowing about it. The thing was, though, as I looked at the envelope, in his rush it seemed he hadn't put the right postage on it, so when it was returned to his college address— where obviously he was no longer living—It must have just sat around until someone there found it, and then I guess tried to send it to us, only this time they had put the wrong address on it for us, so it was returned again, and so on and so forth, until finally being passed here, there and everywhere for months, it eventually ended up coming to our house, and not just to our house—which, given the circumstances, is a bit of a minor miracle in itself—but arriving almost six months afterward at the very time I was sitting there, saying, 'if only I could see him again.' So you can imagine my reaction. It was really like the universe had given me the greatest gift, as if I was being told, 'See, he's still here. You can go on. Who Todd was to everyone continues. His life isn't over. Here he is. He's dead but he is still alive, in a way.'"

I smiled at Charlotte and said, as gently as I could to her, "The universe, maybe, but in fact, Todd himself that sent you the envelope and the pictures and the note. *He's* actually the one who is saying in a much more personal way and directly to you, after his death, 'See, I am still here. Here I am. I'm gone but also not gone. The place I have in your life did not end with my death.'"

She took this in quietly and said, "I don't know to this day what would have shaken me out of it, if I hadn't gotten that letter and those pictures from him, if I hadn't had the chance to see him again in those photos. That incident was definitely the turning point for me emotionally, and slowly, things got better after that, not good, never good, I don't think any parent ever recovers fully from losing a child, but the coincidence of those pictures brought his death and life together for me in a way that was like competing a circle. And from that point, I was able to go on."

In Charlotte's story, as with Carl and Robyn, a synchronistic event happens at just the right time and in just the right way to provide someone grieving a certain kind of completion and an opening to somehow moving on after the death of a loved one. Each story is unique, of course, but I've been surprised to hear from many people about just how often this transition—completing the past and opening to the future, a key part of the mourning process—as accompanied by an unexpected coincidence that happens by pure chance.

When I consider all of these stories about the meaningful coincidences that cluster about the passing of our loved ones—be they preparatory or consolatory, immediate or revealed--I cannot help but hear the plaintive, simple voice of Johnny Cash, singing one of the many songs he became most identified with: "Will the circle be unbroken, by and by, Lord, by and by?" As he goes about preparing himself to attend his mother's funeral, the man in the song asks that question we all ask ourselves when death disrupts our life. Over and over he asks it, a haunting, profound refrain, a open, painful question, and though there is no answer, the stories I've lived and have been told which here make up this final chapter of this imply both "no"—and "yes."

No, the circle of our wholeness will not be unbroken in the course of our life. Broken it will be, for each of us, and that intimate, powerful, abiding physical bond that gave us life and which we live in the bosom of our families will come to an end for every one of us, no exception. But at the same time, what I find most moving about these stories of synchronicities around the deaths of family members is that, *yes,* they provide to the question in Johnny Cash's refrain. Yes, the circle of our lives *will* remain unbroken. The spiritual and emotional bond of family ties abides in ways that transcend time and space—indeed, that is almost the essential nature of the family as a historical and personal reality.

Conclusion

It isn't entirely by chance that these stories of family member's deaths bring this book itself to close, for they are an eminently appropriate conclusion to our much larger and more comprehensive exploration of synchronicity and family relationships. In all the ways that these curious and sometimes dramatic family stories demonstrate, I hope the transcendent nature of the family becomes clear. Rooted as our experience of family is, not just in blood ties to our relatives, but psychologically and emotionally grounded in the deep archetypal level of our common human experience, our families tie together for us time and eternity. And in our family experience, past, present and future come together as a single unitary whole which, if we are paying attention—and sometimes even we are not—a striking synchronistic event may well be brought to our conscious attention.

But that is the key: consciousness. And that is my real purpose in writing this book. Rather than slumber through our experience within our families, taking it for granted or thinking about our relationships as merely conditioned by biological chance or social tradition, I've been struck by how synchronicity wakes us all up to a consciousness of our connectedness. In my life and in the family stories of those who so graciously opened their lives to me for this book, the message seems obvious: we need to bring our awareness actively, thoughtfully, and openly to the events of our lives. Not always, and maybe not even all that frequently, but now and then and very significantly, by random chance, a synchronistic event provides us the opportunity to be aware of the transcendent nature of our love for those with whom we share our lives and our history.

In such meaningful coincidences, we are given a glimpse of the eternal life that our families represent. If we let ourselves see this truth, and let it resonate in our souls, then, and only then, by living our lives in the light of consciousness, does the circle remain unbroken for us. And that is when the stories of our families become the place where the meaning of who we are is born. Then and only then, do we see fully how the scattered and unexpected pieces of our lives can be fashioned into a heart and soul, for ourselves, for our loved ones and for all our descendants.

Auden, W. H. "Twelve Songs: IX, Funeral Blues," 1940. *W. H. Auden Collected Poems.* New York Random House, 2007.

Bolen, Jean Shinoda. *The Tao of Psychology: Synchronicity and the Self.* New York: Harper & Row, 1979.

Boardwalk Pictures, producer. "Chef's Table: Massimo Bottura," Season 1, Episode 1, 2015.

Eliot, T. S. "Little Gidding," *Four Quartets.* New York: Mariner Books, 1968.

Franz, Marie-Louise von. *On Divination and Synchronicity: The Psychology of Meaningful Chance.* Toronto: Inner City Books, 1980.

Hopcke, Robert H.. "Synchronicity in analysis: various types and their roles for patient and analyst." *Quadrant*, 1988, 22(1).

_____.*A Guided Tour of the "Collected Works" of C. G. Jung.* Boston: Shambhala Publications, 1989, 2nd edition, 1999.

_____."On the Threshold of Change: Synchronistic Events and Their Liminal Context in Analysis." In Stein, Murray (ed.), *Liminality and Transitional Space in Analysis.* Chicago: Chiron Publications, 1990.

_____."The Barker: A Synchronistic Event in Analysis." *Journal of Analytical Psychology*, Spring, 1991.

_____.*There Are No Accidents: Synchronicity and the Stories of Our Lives.* New York: Riverhead Books, 1997.

_____."Synchronicity and Psychotherapy: Jung's Concept and Its Use in Clinical Work." *Psychiatric Annals*, Volume 39, Issue 5, May, 2009.

I Ching or Book of Changes, third edition, translated by Richard Wilhelm. Princeton: Princeton University Press, 1967.

Jung, C. G. "On the Psychology and Pathology of So-Called Occult Phenomena," 1902, in vol. 1 of *The Collected Works of C. G. Jung*. Princeton: Princeton University Press, 1978.

_____. *Psychological Types,* 1921 Volume 6 of *The Collected Works of C. G. Jung*. Princeton: Princeton University Press, 1971.

_____. "On Psychic Energy," 1948. In vol. 8 of *The Collected Works of C. G. Jung*. Princeton: Princeton University Press, 1960.

_____. "The Psychology of Eastern Meditation," 1948, in vol. 11, of *The Collected Works of C. G. Jung*. Princeton: Princeton University Press, 1975.

_____. "Foreword to the *I Ching*," 1950, in vol. 11, of *The Collected Works of C. G. Jung*. Princeton: Princeton University Press, 1975.

_____. "On Synchronicity," 1952, in vol. 8 of *The Collected Works of C. G. Jung*. Princeton: Princeton University Press, 1960.

_____. *Synchronicity: An Acausal Connecting Principle*, 1952, in vol. 8 of *The Collected Works of C. G. Jung*. Princeton: Princeton University Press, 1960.

_____. "An Astrological Experiment," 1958, in vol. 18, of *The Collected Works of C. G. Jung*. Princeton: Princeton University Press, 1980.

_____. *Memories, Dreams, Reflections.* New York: Vintage Books, 1965.

Strabala, David, director (documentary film). *What is Synchronicity?* 2014.

About the Author

Robert H. Hopcke is a licensed Marriage, Family and Child Counselor in private practice in Berkeley, California. Along with his numerous articles and reviews published over the last 30 years, his national best-seller, *There Are No Accidents: Synchronicity and the Stories of Our Lives*, has been popular throughout the world and since been translated into a dozen different languages. Known for his landmark work in  Jungian psychology on issues of human sexuality and social justice such as *Jung, Jungians and Homosexuality; Men's Dreams, Men's Healing; A Guided Tour of the Collected Works of C. G. Jung;* and *The Persona: Where Sacred Meets Profane,* he is currently on the clinical faculty of Pacific Center for Human Growth where serves as supervisor, and has been enjoying an active career as translator of works on spirituality and religion from the Italian, including a contemporary American English rendition of The Little Flowers of St. Francis of Assisi.

CPSIA information can be obtained
at www.ICGtesting.com
Printed in the USA
FFHW021703270319
51244487-56782FF

9 781630 514884